God Is Able

T0208425

God Is Able

Shimeka S. Brown

iUniverse, Inc.
New York   Bloomington

GOD IS ABLE

*THE HOLY BIBLE NIV   Copyright 2006 by The Zondervan
Corporation*

iUniverse books may be ordered through booksellers or by contacting:

*iUniverse
1663 Liberty Drive
Bloomington, IN 47403
www.iuniverse.com
1-800-Authors (1-800-288-4677)*

*Because of the dynamic nature of the Internet, any Web addresses or
links contained in this book may have changed since publication and may
no longer be valid.*

*ISBN: 978-1-4401-7342-4 (sc)
ISBN: 978-1-4401-7343-1 (ebk)*

Printed in the United States of America

iUniverse rev. date: 4/6/2010

Introduction

God is able! When I first started writing this book, I was not strong in the word as I am now. When I was writing this book, I was convicted of God's word. When I was writing this book, I experienced trials and tribulations as I wrote these prayers. When I wrote this book, I felt like giving up. When I wrote this book, I was not of the human flesh, God was writing through me. I am not worthy of the things I said in this book. He speaks through me. I thank God that he used me through my talent to reach out to others. Sometimes we get so caught up in our talents and our gifts that we forget that Jesus is the reason for our season. He gives us our identity. Everything works together for the good of God and those who are called according to his purpose. I've been reading the word and experiencing life's difficulties and the happiness of obeying our Savior! It is a feeling you have to feel for yourself. Some days I can't believe how I minister to others and keep my strength. I know today that my help always came from the Lord. When we put our trust in the Lord and not mankind, he will reveal a source of power that is so real that we have to believe. Our faith carries us through this life, Romans 10"17 states, "Faith comes by hearing and hearing by the word of GOD." Mother, father, sister, brother, friend, co worker, lover and cousins can't replace the love of Christ. Christ isolates us from everything sometimes so that we can call upon him and praise him. Encourage yourself to the Lord. You shouldn't have to wait until Sunday Morning service to glorify God. When he wakes you up, that's a miracle. I have learned so much writing this book that my little brain will never be able to comprehend. However, God has a way of speaking to me that no one can. I've often been that strength for my family and friends to make it through the night. I have been going through tribulations with my own family as well. However, we all need to know as individuals, it's not about us or the people in our life, it's about God. If he doesn't do anything for you tomorrow, you need to glorify him for what he's done in your past and what he's done today. Your salvation is already in heaven! His arms will be wide open for you on that Glorious day! Like my pastor says, "That's good news!" Saints all I'm saying is don't give up or feel discouraged because a storm is coming. God said, "Be still and know that I am GOD." I hope at least one prayer reaches out to someone as they read this book today. Remember no matter what you go through in life, GOD IS ABLE!

Dedication

This book is dedicated to Melvin and Lillian Collins as well as Cecila Payne. May Melvin and Lillian Rest In Peace. My grandparents both passed away before my high school graduation. However, their legacy and roots live on. I am reminded today of the song, "But I had a praying Grandmother." Life takes us through so much as we grow and make our way in this cruel world. However, it is the elderly people that have wisdom that prays daily for us and read the word of God for their source of strength. As a young adult we sometimes fail to go to God for our source of power and strength. Many times if it was not for our grandparents we would not be where we are today. I truly believe the same is for myself. Life will take us all through twist and turns. Mostly parents are the ones who are going through trials and tribulations and are trying to find God's love in the midst. The grandparents are the ones who have been there and done that, and know that life will let you down without the love of Christ. My grandmother was one of those women. I remember how she kept her mind stayed on Jesus! Even when things seem rough she would read her bible. I remember as a young child she would get on her knees every night and pray. I didn't understand it at the time, but she was praying for me! She was praying for her family. Even when it would storm outside she taught me to keep my bible open and under my pillow. She told me that it would "cut the storm." Some may not believe it, but as a child who is severely scared of bad weather, it helps me today. My grandmother taught me to lay on the word of God in the midst of the storms and that is what's keeping me today. If you have elders in your life today that you tend to ignore or overlook, be advised that GOD is using them to bless you. Love on your grandparents and parents today. Love on your mentors that have experienced life. Seek wisdom from your elders in the church today. They may not be able to walk like you walk or talk like you talk but the kind of peace that they can pray for your life and your children's life is far more important than any riches that this life can bring. I still have one grandmother alive today, Cecila Payne and she is a humble and kind woman. When people speak of her, if they ever passed her in their travels, they will be able to say, that woman had the peace of God inside of her. God is able and I thank him for elderly people.

Contents

God is Able   1

A Prayer for your Future (A brighter future through the Promise of God)   4

A Prayer for Child Discipline(I love you so much it hurts)   7

A Prayer for Encouragement(I know I am the child of GOD)   11

A Prayer for Fear (If I Fear God Nothing Else Matters)   15

A Prayer for Financial Deliverance (My Father is my Provider)   19

A Prayer for Honesty (Tell the Truth and Shame the Devil)   23

A Prayer for Hope (The Holy Spirit has its benefits)   27

A Prayer for Keeping God's Will(Not as I Will but As You Will)   33

A Prayer for Laziness(The Work is Plenty)   39

A Prayer for Peace of Mind(Lord Align My Mind with my Heart)   44

A Prayer for Strength (One Day at a Time)   48

A Prayer for Work (When God Is With you who can be against you)   52

A Prayer for the End of Time (Tomorrow Is Not
    Promised)   56

A Prayer for the Sick (A Doctor in the Sick Room)   62

A Wife's Prayer (Thank God for My Wife)   65

A Prayer for Seeking God (And If I be lifted up from
    this Earth)   69

A Prayer for Keeping God in your Home (As for Me
    and My House)   73

A Prayer for Relationships (Be Not Unequally Yoked) 76

A Prayer for Trusting in the Lord (Be Still and Know
    that I am God)   81

A Prayer for self-renewal (Change My Heart O Lord) 85

A Prayer for Standing on God's word alone (Father I
    Stretch My Hands to thee)   90

A Prayer for Fellowship (Fellowship)   95

A Prayer for Forgiving Others (Forgiving Others)   100

A Prayer for Parental Obedient (Honoring Parents)   104

A Prayer for Worship (How Excellent)   110

A Prayer for Loving (I Want to Know What Love Is) 113

A Prayer for Proper family Separation (Knowing When
    to Walk Away)   118

A Prayer for seeking Heaven (In My Father's House) 122

A Prayer to for Complaining (Oh Lord I Won't
    Complain)   125

A Prayer for religious foundation (Old Time
    Religion)   129

A Prayer for Raising Children (Just to be Close to
    you)   132

A Prayer for Leadership (The Power of Godly
    Leadership)   137

A Prayer for your thoughts (Seeds Planted in the
    Soul)   140

A Prayer for Serving God (Serving God Alone)   144

A Prayer for Your Trials (Suffering For Christ)   147

A Prayer for Grieving (The Heavenly Journal)   151

A Prayer for seeking a church home (The Lord's
    House)   156

A Prayer for Endurance (The Race of Life)   159

A Prayer for Praying (The Silent Prayer)   163

A Prayer for Sinning (The Toolbox to Jesus)   168

A Prayer for Doing God's Will (The Will of God)   172

A Prayer for Celebrating God's Victory (Victory is
    Mine)   174

A Prayer for God's Presence in Your Life (Welcome
    Lord)   177

A Prayer for Marriage (When A Man Findeth A
    Wife)   180

A Prayer for Steadfast (When the World Forgets
    Me)   186

A Poem for Guidance (Why)   190

A Prayer for Women (Women of Christ)   195

A Prayer for Worrying (Worrying)   200

I Wish I'd Known Jesus (Poem)   206

He's Able

There were times when I didn't want to get out of bed, there were times when I lost people that were dear to me, but I still continued on about my day. I woke up, I went to work, although I may not be as joyous as I was on other days, I still gave my co-workers that laugh and that smile, because although I mourn, they still may need it. I've had a co-worker tell me, "No matter what you go through, you still come to work smiling, and it gives me hope." It feels good to know that you give others hope. I just feel like this is the least I can do because God gave his only begotten son for us. At times we don't appreciate what he's done for us because we are so busy trying to find our way through life without him when all we have to do is call upon him. An old gospel song said, "Jesus is on the mainline tell him what you want." As human beings we just don't realize how easy it is to just call upon him. His word is written and it is done, our ticket to heaven is guaranteed. A poem for inspiration. God is Able!

MATTHEW 14:36

"And besought him that they might only touch the hem of his garment: and as many as touched were made perfectly whole."

Put your trust in the Lord today
As you follow his will.
He will protect you from danger
and when you are sick,
he will definitely heal.

Have no worries about
which way to turn
when the bills are due.
God has it all figured out
for me and you.
When we are sleep he
is working things out in
Heaven.
When we only have a dollar
In our pocket he will
multiply it times seven.

God is a good God and he
has the power to change
what we can not.
So trust God's word
and be a witness
so others can learn
what his mercy is
all about.

Rejoice in the hour
Of trouble as your
enemies laugh.
God is able to
fool the devil
and cut his wicked
ways in half.

All you need is
four simple things,
Faith, Love, hope,
and always use the bible
as your guide,
the word of God is
a must.

He's a miracle worker
always bringing blessings
to our table.
Give the praise to God,
he's real, he's mighty
and he's able!
AMEN

A Brighter Future Through The Promise of God

Have you ever been there? Have you ever been alone or in the dark? Have you ever felt like you were sinking deep in sin and there was no life vest around? Well I surely have. I've been at a point in my life where if it had not been for the Lord on my side I would not be here today. Many times we feel as if we can walk the walk and talk the talk by ourselves. We think that we know what's best for us. However, Jesus said he is of the heavens and not the earth. We are of the earth so our way of thinking is earthly, but his way of thinking is high as the heavens. He can see that in which we can't and if we don't allow him to be our guidance in life, we are walking in a valley of death because we don't see the danger ahead. I've noticed that friends and family come into your life at certain points, but there comes a time when no one will be around and you will be isolated. You must know that Jesus is always with you, even though you can't see him, he's there. Many times I would make foolish decisions and I would put my life in danger, but because I always pray for his protection, Jesus is always with me. He can bring you out and he can build you up and set

your path so high that no man can touch you. Jesus will lift
you and shine a light inside of you that will lead you out of
the pit of guilt. Don't just say it, but pray this prayer for your
strength in God as you search for a brighter future.

Jeremiah 29:11

*"For I know the plans I have for you." declares the
LORD, "plans to prosper you and not to harm you,
plans to give you hope and a future."*

Dear God,
Please help me to understand
You have a plan for my life.
Show me that these troubles
Don't last always, this
Pain and strife.

Oh Father,
When I want to hold on
to things that are not
good for me,
help me to realize
by doing so I'm blocking
my blessings.

Father God,
Teach me your will
Because mine is not
Working out at all.
When I try to do it by
Myself, I constantly
Fall.

Others try to

Tell me I'm not
Worthy of
Your grace,
Because of my sins,
And that I should
Have a broken back
And shameful face.

 "Thou I walk
Through the valley
Of the shadow of
Death, I shall
Fear no evil"
Is what you said.
Give me peace
In my heart
Through these tears
I shed.

You said you shall
Make my enemies my
Foot stool.
So when I want to
Do my own thing Lord,
Help me to stay
Calm and cool.
I will stand on your
Word through and through,
For you said it,
"I have plans to prosper
You and not harm you."
AMEN

I Love You So Much It Hurts

"What's wrong with you? You the only one in your class that can't write your words! Are you retarded?" This may be so sad reading, but something that is so true. This is how I talked to my child in Kindergarten. As a single mom in the military I worked long hours and I had my cross to bear. When it came time to do homework at night, I had too much on my mind my patience was zero. Shame on me, shame on me for not taking time away from the problems of my world and give that energy to my son. Sometimes life takes us through twist and turns until we get lost. I turned to the church and learned that kids are only who we make them. They learn from us. If my son was lacking, it was because I was lacking. When I took time out to teach him, he learned. When I spend time with my son, he would behave appropriately. Sometimes kids act up in school and in public because they are really screaming for attention. It's more to raising kids than just providing food and shelter. A baby is hungry for knowledge and love, just as Christians who are born again and looking for blessings through Christ. That's why it is good to walk with God before you have kids because if not, you are going to have problems within yourself and you will find it difficult to be that parent that a child needs. Know that children don't ask to come into this world. They only know what we teach and give them. I love my son so much. I used to let him get away with certain things because I was just too tired to discipline him. I was at home alone with him, and going to his room and watching his DVD was just too convenient for me. Oh, but low and behold when I was in public and he acted badly, I was saying, "What's wrong with this boy?" When we spend time with our kids and play with them and bond with them, discipline will fall in place. However, kids will be kids and they will always try to get away with things but you have to put, what my mom would call, "fire," in their soul. Just like we have the fear of God in us, our kids need the fear of "mommy and daddy in them." One thing I always remembered was that my mom she would always pray that God would put her children around people that were blessings to them. That to me was so powerful! Powerful because she admits that her kids will go through trials and tribulations, but she knew with God on their side, that they would make it through anything. Bless her soul today for that. Whatever your situation is today with your kids, or step-kids, know that God is working it out and he has a plan. Do not be afraid to discipline them. They will not grow to hate you. Your kids know your heart as well as God. Pray this prayer for your strength in the Lord as you raise your child according to God's will. God is able!

Proverbs 23:13

"Do not withhold discipline from a child; if you punish him with the rod, he will not die."

Heavenly Father,
I pray that you will
Give me the courage to
Discipline my daughter/son.
May I be

Consistent in
Teaching and
Spending time
With my little
One.

Father some days
Are long and work
Can wear me down!
But keep us alert
As parents,
when danger
Is lurking around.

Help me to
Understand that
It's the little
Things we
Have to catch
At an early age.
Comfort me today
Lord because
I know he will
Go through
That rebellious
Phase.

Oh Lord, just
Keep me patient
As I teach
Him the right way!
May I constantly,
Discipline him
When he goes
Astray.

Oh Father,
help all
The parents
Who are
Struggling
With their
Kids today.
Reveal to them
That there is
A
Time to laugh,
Joke, cry,
Be serious
And a time
To pray.

Father
We know that
A child can
Bring us
Shame,
Right before
Our very eyes.
Your word states,
"Do not withhold discipline
from a child;
If you punish him
with the rod,
 he will not die"
AMEN

I Know I am the Child of God

I'm reminded of a song today, "Sometimes You have to Encourage Yourself". There may come a time in your life when nothing or no one will agree with you, no one will answer your cry or they may simply reject your wisdom and faith in the Lord. Whether it be family, friends or co-workers, know that God is in you and that's all you need when you go through storms and trials. Sometimes you have to speak words of encouragement to yourself. You are a child of God. Jesus died so that you can live a blessed and graceful life. You can do all things through Christ who strengthens you. Do not be discouraged by what others say to you. You have been renewed through Christ Jesus and Victory is in his name! Nothing or no one can touch you! Be all that you can be today and tomorrow because when we walk in faith and confidence he shines a light inside of us for others to see. You are more than a conqueror! A man does not make you if you are a woman, a woman does not make you if you are a man, your kids do not determine your faith, your parents can't tell you your worth, God said it so you believe it and you speak words of encouragement in that mirror today. Genesis said it all; he made man in the image and likeness of him. Imagine being like God. That's good news. God loves you more than you love yourself. Receive him today. When you go to bed at night, you have to sleep with yourself. When you wake up and look in the mirror it is yourself that you see. Love yourself; embrace yourself today Children of Israel! Greater is he that is within ME than he who is in this world. Take a vow to honor yourself today because you are a child of God. Do not let your past define you, do not let other people who are intimidating define you, do not let your habits or your physical being define you, let Jesus Christ who works within you, who's mercy is sufficient, let him have the final say in your thoughts today. Pray this prayer for your strength in Encouragement today. God is able.

GENESIS 1:26

"Let Us make man in Our image, according to Our likeness;"

Dear God,
I pray for those today who
fail to see their worth.
Those who fail to see
they were made perfect
from birth.

I pray for those who
have low self-esteem
because of others.
Show everyone father,
you made us alike,
as sisters and brothers.

Our images and likeness
are colorful and true,
but Heavenly father,
we all are a reflection of you.

How blessed we are to
carry a part of you everyday
in this life.
God once we realize this,
we will become better
Christians, mothers,
fathers, husbands
and wives.

Teach someone today
Lord, that there
is nothing that they
cannot do.
For we were
created with
power so that
we might be a joy to you.

That lonely girl who
feels she needs a man
to make her great,
Father show her,
she was made in
your image
and give her faith.

Father cover
the deaf and the blind
with your love and
kindness as we speak.
Give them the strength
and the courage to make
it through a rough week.

Father we all go
through things and wonder
why it had to happen to us.
Help us to be prayerful,
patient and in your word
continue to trust.

Many struggle with weight,
height or even racial criticism
on this earth.
Father forgive us for
forgetting how much
our lives are worth.

Dear God,
re-new yourself in our
lives today.
Father we know
your word is faithful
and true.
From the beginning
of time,
you made us in the
image and likeness
of you.
AMEN

If I Fear God Nothing Else Matters

"Yea, though I walk through the valley of the shadow of death, I will fear no evil: For thou art with me;

Thy rod and thy staff, they comfort me." I don't preach to others and try to make them walk the exact path I walk, but I just try to live my life in a way that they may see how GOD is blessing me and want the same for themselves. GOD said, "Let your light shine so bright before men that they may see your good works and acknowledge me." I've found it disturbing that people I met in life try to make others believe they are so saved and that their lives are so perfect and try to tell others what they need to do for Jesus. Truly if you are a child of GOD you don't have to say a word, your life speaks for itself. Telling someone how to serve GOD is not Christian like because Jesus talks to us individually and tells us how to serve him. When we go through difficult times in our life God is with us. He may have others say things to us to trigger that spiritual feeling inside, but he has a way of communicating with us that man can not. I thank GOD I know his voice. I know the voice of Jesus and when he's talking to me. He may have to shake me, and if the whispering doesn't work, he knows how to yell at me, but he knows me he knows my heart and I know his presence and purpose in my life. I know my help comes from the Lord and my strength too. God has not given us the spirit of fear. You may be going through something today and it seems as if no one is around. No one will answer your calls or cries. Know that God is able and he knows our hearts. We don't have to worry or fear others or things that are beyond our control because he is working it out today. If God is for us, who can be against us? I'm reminded today, though I walk through the valley of the shadow of death, I shall fear no evil, for thou are with me. Pray this prayer for strength in the Lord as you learn to Fear God and all other fears shall cease. He's able.

2 TIMOTHY 1:7

"For God hath not given us the spirit of fear; but of power, and of love, and of a sound mind"

Dear God,
Help me to walk with confidence
as I do your will.
Although I am not sure
what's on the other side of that hill.

Father you said the holy
spirit resides in me.
 It is through you
I can visualize all things
the human eyes
cannot see.

It is through your
love that the enemy
will continue to

fail!
It is through you
that my soul
is safe from
bondage and hell!

God you said in
your word that you
will give us understanding
and wisdom.
Glory be to you God,
I can fight this battle
when evil comes!

Glory be to you God
for keeping my mind
sound and alert!
Glory be to you
that I can recover
when my body
aches and hurt!

Dear God,
I know that there
are other sisters and
brothers afraid today.
Crying and praying
for you to carry their
burdens away.

May we forever
stand on your word
as you send blessings
from heaven above.
Father you said,

"I have not given you
the spirit of fear, but of
power and love..."
AMEN

My Father Is My Provider

Many times we feel as if giving a dollar or two during church service will deliver us from all of our financial burdens. Many times we feel as if we give money to the church that it is going towards things in which we do not wish to contribute. Many times we feel as if we do not have to give anything, yet we expect something from GOD (blessings and deliverance). I've always heard people say, "God knows my heart. He knows I don't have it." My pastor has always been a firm believer that "We spend most of our time, unlearning things than actually learning." God loves you regardless of who you are and what you have. Know that God watches where we spend our money and our energy. Why not spend your money and energy in the church because you will spend it in the restaurant? You will be faithful when you give a good waitress a tip. God does so much for you; you should be pouring out riches to him. He knows our heart, and when we give, we need to do so from our heart. There are many churches that are growing in ministry as well as building space and recreation for the members. When you give to the church, you are contributing to the recreation and blessings that come from social events and praise services. When you give to the church, you are telling God, "You have been so good to me, you gave your life, the least I can do is pay 10%" Many may say, "I don't have it to give. If I give the church 10% I will only have 100 dollars left for the week." I am here to say, God sits high but he looks low. Psalms 37:16 states, "A little that a righteous man has Is better than the riches of many wicked". He knows your bills, he knows your struggles and he knows your heart. If you are faithful and obedient in your giving God will deliver you financially. Malachi 3:10 states, "Then you will see that I will throw open the windows of heaven. I will pour out so many blessings that you will not have enough room for them." He will make a way out of no way. Sometimes you may not see your way out of a financial burden but God will deliver you. He just wants to know that you are a giving person. He wants to know that you not only want to receive the blessings you have for him, but that you are willing to be a blessing to others. Giving to the church is a blessing but also doing for other people. When you allow people in your life and home in order to provide support for them that is another form of giving. Giving is sacrificial. If you sacrifice your time and money in order to help your sisters and brothers in Christ, you are giving from your heart. Never be too high and mighty where you can't help someone in need. Additionally, just because you lack financially don't turn your back on people. You may only have two dollars, but your brother or sister that is in need should have one of those dollars. Pray this prayer for your deliverance in the Lord as you ask for strength in your giving. God is Able!

Philippians 4:19

"And my God will meet all your needs according to his glorious riches in Christ Jesus"

Dear God,
I have made some bad choices in my past,
causing me to suffer today.

I have allowed bills to pile up and
there are many more on its way.

Every time I think I will get
a break and see the road to
success ahead,
Something always sets
my bank account in
the negative instead.

Father help me to be
faithful in paying my
tithes in church.
All you ask for is 10%
so I should at least
pay you first.

Help me to discipline
myself in purchasing items
I do not need.
Often times we want
to be like our neighbors
and our eyes envy with greed.

Teach me the way O Lord,
to deposit myself in the word
and all that it gives.
Order my steps today so that
I don't have to worry about
tomorrow as long as I live.

For father you said,
If we just serve you
and tell others of your
Glory throughout the day,

You shall add these things
unto us as we follow
your ways.

I know to the flesh,
my situation seems
impossible and hard
to reverse.
Father I know your
power is higher
than our earthly
ways and you
will break this curse.

You said,
"Ask and you shall
receive, seek and you
shall find"
In your name Jesus,
touch this financial
situation of mine.

If ever there was
a place of comfort
father, your
word is sure to
please us,
As it is written,
"And my God will meet all your needs according
to his glorious riches in Christ Jesus."
AMEN

Tell The Truth and Shame The Devil

Have you ever seen one of your family members that were just so excited about their new hairstyle? They call you on the way home and tell you that you are just going to love it! They open the door with the biggest smile on their face! When you come around the corner in anticipation of the new him or her your heart drops as you find an awful style. You pause for a moment to collect your thoughts. Your first instinct tells you to put on this fake smile and say, "Oh, yeah, that's nice." However, it takes everything inside of you to hold back how you really feel. You want to say, "What on earth? Do you not see what I see?" Or maybe you have been in a bad financial situation. You know you have a problem saving money. Women, I know some of you can vouch for this too. You have bills that are overdue. Maybe you have an addiction that you are not honest about because you don't want them to look at you in a certain way. Instead of telling your husband/wife, the truth about your problem or addictions, you make them think that everything is okay. You do this because you don't want your faults to be a major problem in your relationship. Let's be honest, you don't want them to look at you differently or leave you. All these things are common when we walk in the human flesh. However, we fail to realize that the lies start to consume us. If that hairstyle is really ugly, think about it, you have to walk around and look at that mess all day. It's a way that you can be gentle and true, instead of dishonest with a smile. When you let that financial problem or addiction go too far, instead of protecting them with your lies, you end up hurting them worse in the end. They feel like, "Not only did they lie to me, but now this problem is so big it's going to take a while to overcome." We fail to realize if we are honest from the start, then it would save a lot of pain and tears. God said love is true. God is the truth. Sometimes we don't want to do what GOD has called us to do, but God does not change his will for us because we don't like it. It stays the same. His word is never changing. Yet his truth is love. He loves us unconditionally. No matter what our faults are he opens his arms to us. If people in your life only love you because of the good things that you do, then you do not need them in your life. We all have faults. None of us are perfect. If we were, Jesus would not have came down from heaven and saved our souls. Spend more time loving yourself and being truthful to yourself and God, and then you will be able to see those who wish to destroy you or love you. We have to love one another just the same. God said, (John 15, should be read in its entirety to grasp the meaning of this) "Love others as I have loved you, and by this they will know that you are my child." Pray this prayer for your strength in the Lord as you learn to become an honest person to yourself, God, and the people you love. God is able!

Ephesians 4:15

*"Instead, we will speak the truth in love, growing in
every way more and more like Christ, who is the head
of his body, the church"*

Dear God,
So often we try to please others
with our slick tongue and ways.
Thinking we can gain the love we need
to make the pain go away.

God your love is true and it does
not hurt others at all.
Father teach us today that being
truthful to ourselves is the first
step to breaking down the devil's wall.

God once we are truthful to ourselves,
then we can be truthful to one another.
Father teach us today that we don't have
to lie to gain the love of our sisters and brothers.

If others can't accept us for whom we are, then
they have to answer to you.
Father teach us to be faithful in our work, family
and in everything we do.

If we lie to ourselves and others, we try to deceive
our father in heaven.
You see straight through us like an eye on a sparrow.

But when we come to you in truth, you can hear
us and respond.
You are the truth and the light, giving salvation
to everyone.

You are that strength that will help us forget about
the truthful pain.
You are that strength that will keep us from
withholding the truth again and again.

How easy it is to say what others want to hear.
We allow it to manifest in our souls that
the truth becomes unclear.

Heavenly father you said in your word,
"We will speak the truth growing
in every way, more and more in Christ"
Give us the strength today to
be truthful in love instead of
being looked at as a dishonest nice.
Amen.

The Holy Spirit Has Its Benefits

Have you ever gone to the grocery store one day after work when the line was so long you felt like walking away, but you didn't? Perhaps you were in traffic when you needed to make it to the airport and you only had 30 minutes to get there? You could have given up and said I'm not going to make it, but that one day you were determined and you made it? God has a way of showing up and showing out when we think the impossible is before us. Have you ever had a bill to pay and they said you had 48 hours and you knew there was no way? You didn't give up but you searched for a way to make the payment. God made a way out of no way. Even in our country today, many leaders have no clue of how they are going to accomplish a certain goal. However, they say to the people, "We will get through this", but inside they don't know the answers. This is called having hope. As long as you have that urge inside of you to make it through, you can do anything. Hope builds faith and gives you the passion you need to do the impossible. God is working it out when we don't have a clue. God is healing when we pray that he can do so. God is fixing what is broken when we are trying to put the pieces together. God is carrying you when you feel like you can't make it on your own. All you have to do is have an ounce of hope in your body and he will do the rest. God's word is written. Everything that he said would happen, has happened, is happening and will happen tomorrow. He said nor would he leave you or forsake you. He hasn't proven to do so yet. If we want Jesus to work through us, we have to invite him into our lives and take control of our troubles. Don't try to do things on your own because it will discourage you and you will loose focus. Remember in the bible when Jesus told Peter to come to him. Peter started walking in the water, but then he was discouraged by the wind. Because of his fear, he lost focus on Jesus and started to drown. When we loose focus of his word we begin to drown in these earthly ways. Keep your mind stayed on Jesus even when others try to pull you from one side to the other. Know your purpose and know that God can and he will. He said it in his word and you have to believe. Having hope, are inviting miracles and faith producing testimonies in your life today that you may be able to share to others and bring glory to his name. Pray this prayer for your strength in having hope, which is one of the benefits of God's holy spirit today. God is able.

ROMANS 15:4

"For whatsoever things were written aforetime were written for our learning, that we through patience and comfort of the scriptures might have hope"

Dear God,
Please plant in my
soul, your holy word
as I read it every morn.
The miracles and prayers
written saved my
life even

before I was
born.

Father I know
that if I confess
my sins and
believe,
I can move
a mountain
and cast it into
the sea.

Father I know
that if I just
have faith in you,
I can be healed
like that woman
in Gadarnes
who touched
your garment
through faith too.

Father I know
that if I seek
your kingdom first,
you said all things
shall be added unto
me.
So I will not worry
about the convictions
of this world,
for in Christ Jesus,
my soul is free!

I will proclaim your
name, all the days
of my life Oh Lord!
I will praise you
like King David,
in thanksgiving
and when times get
hard.

I will be mindful
of the life I
live in order to
glorify
your
unconditional
 love.
When and if I
 deny you like
Peter did,
may I confess
my sins to heaven
above.

It is written
that we should
love others
as you have loves
us.
May we have a
forgiving heart
and in
in you,
place our trust.

I will pray
for others in
private
and
you will reward
me
for doing so.
May I be
cleansed
with your
word as you
tell me to
"go and sin no more!"

Oh Father God,
so much was written,
all to give us
comfort in the
holy spirit!
The scriptures
of the old and
new Testament,
may I continuously
hear it
and
feel it!

Dear God,
when I'm lost on
my way,
I shall feed
my soul your
word and pray!

As a child of
God, my heart
has a passion
for the word
as well as
a yearning.
Father you said,
"For whatsoever things were written aforetime
were written for our learning."
  AMEN

Not As I Will But As You Will

Matthew 7:13-14

"Enter ye in at the strait gate: for wide is the gate, and broad is the way, that leadeth to destruction, and many there he which go in thereat: Because strait is the gate, and narrow is the way, which leadeth unto life, and few there be that find it." Many times we want what our friends have and we want certain people to stay in our lives forever, however GOD said that our path of righteousness is a personal choice. The things in which someone else own may not be God's will for you because he knows each of our hearts and our desires. GOD said "Where your treasure is, there your heart will be also" Some of us can't handle riches without it changing the type of person we are. Some of us don't know Jesus until we are down to our last dollar and meal. It may take some of us being broken and bent to humble ourselves before him. Jesus wants us to focus on ourselves, loving who we are and appreciating the things in which we have in life because in heaven we will all be equal. Our focus is on that narrow walk. We may feel like it's a lonely walk because many are not following this path, but GOD will put a joy inside of us that is so powerful that we will never feel lonely again. Prayer and faith will guide you through and when you feel like you are tired and weak, the bible and the church is your strength, it is your reference. Look ever forward and know that you are never alone. Sometimes we have to let go of things that hinder us from taking that walk with God. It's hard to let go of things that are in the flesh but we can do all things through Christ. Although the road may seem rough, he gives us peace in the midst of the storm and we find strength we didn't know we had. Life is full of destruction and pain which is so easy to fall victim of but God said "Greater is he that is within me than he that is in the world". Meaning God will pick you up and take you away from the storm and gently place you in the position you need to be to Glorify him. Praying and reading the word is the key to this kind of relief. "Broad is the gate and wide is the way that leadeth to destruction many may find it, but Strait is the gate and narrow is the way that leadeth to life, only few will find it". Pray this prayer for Keeping God's will no matter what. God is able.

MATTHEW 7: 13; 14

"Enter ye in at the strait gate:
for wide is the gate, and broad is the way,
that leadeth to destruction,
and many there be which go in thereat:
Because strait is the gate,
and narrow is the way,
which leadeth unto life,
and few there be that find it."

Oh Heavenly Father,
Keep me in your presence
and hear my cry.
Use me to bring
others your way before
I die.

Father I know that
I stray away every now and then,
but I want you to
pull me back on that
path from destruction and sin.

It's so easy to fall
into temptation in
this human flesh,
but God you said
follow you with faith
and you will give my
heart rest.

Lord I want to
do right, and
sometimes it
hurts to do your will.
Help me to bring honor
to your name,
and in doing so
may I keep still!

So many of my
sisters and brothers
lay in agony and pain,
not knowing that if
they just follow you,

they will be able to
live again.

Father,
that narrow path
is calling our name.
help us to let go
of this heavy weight
of fortune and fame.

Dear God,
with my faith
and holy spirit,
I need the armor of
you,
although
a sinful path is
wide,
in the midst of
it all,
your promise
remains true.

I'll walk with my
head high
as I squeeze
through that
 narrow lane.
Your word
brings Glory
and sunshine
during my
struggles and pain.

It's so easy
to give up,
so easy to
let go of
your
commandments
you have in place
for me.
It's so easy
to let the devil
give us the desires
of our heart,
making us think
these are the things
that human eyes need
to see!

Oh Father,
I know that is just
a test that you give
me as your child in Christ,
to see if I have what it takes
to Glorify you and
your son who paid
a powerful price!

I will stay focus,
and when evil
forces enter my
house,
in your name,
I'll bind it!
You said God,
"Because strait is
the gate, and

narrow is the way,
that leadeth unto
life, and
only few will
find it."
AMEN

The Work Is Plenty

So often people grow up with a haunting past. The mother was on drugs, the father was never there. Maybe a child's parents were in jail, or simply the way in which they earned a living was not honest and just. Sometimes all we know is what we were taught. Laziness is a term to describe one's initiative in life but at the same time there is meaning behind why people choose to do little or nothing in life. That's why we put our faith in God. Reading the word everyday will help us see things about ourselves that we don't see. It's easy for someone to tell you that you are lazy but until you see it for yourself you may think that they are jealous or that they are just trying to discourage you. There are people out there today that worked hard once upon a time but give up because they feel as if the work they do is not good enough to fix the problems in their life. However, you need to know that showing initiative and being in the right place at the right time may be where your blessings come from. There are so many of us that do not feel like going to work and dealing with the disgruntle employees and bosses but we do it. Not because we are beneath them, but because we are faithful in the work we do and we know God will provide peace and comfort for us because of our diligence and steadfast honor. People would be so surprise how good it feels to make an honest living everyday. Stealing, killing and getting over on other people just so you can get ahead are laziness and its weakness. God gives us strength in the time of need. Your time of need may be in the work that you do. Don't give up and stumble. God said, "Seek first the kingdom of God and all his righteousness and all these things shall be added unto you." Matthew 6:33. You don't have to look no further than Jesus. You must show Jesus that you are willing to go out there and work hard for what you want and need and he will reward you. Some of us blame others for our faults and downfalls. Jesus is here with arms wide open and no matter your situation he is going to be right there providing for you. If Jesus was lazy, then we would not be saved today. It took time and discipline for him to wake up everyday and go preach the gospel. He went on mountain tops. He went to different lands and countries. He was tired and hungry but he knew the father would make a way out of no way. The least we can do is show some type of initiative instead of blaming our problems on mankind. Flesh will let you down, but the God I serve is a mighty God. Isaiah 40:31 states, "But they that wait upon the LORD shall renew their strength; they shall mount up with wings as eagles; they shall run, and not be weary; and they shall walk, and not faint." When you have that kind of support, why wouldn't you want to work? Pray this prayer for your strength in the lord as you pray for yourself and others who are lazy. God is able!

ROMANS 12:11

"Never be lazy, but work hard and serve the Lord enthusiastically"

Dear God,
 Please encourage someone
to make an honest

living today.
Help them to understand
That hard work is
Necessary to enjoy
The benefits of pay.

Give them the
Drive they need
To get up and go!
A man that supports
His family,
Sets an example
For them to
Physically and
Mentally grow.

Dear God,
Touch all the
Young men at
Home with no desire
to earn a decent living.
Father you said to
Those that give
Much is given.

Show them
Heavenly father,
That their good
Works can bless
Another.
There are those
Who are disabled
And can't
Work to
take care

of their kids and
mothers.

Dear God,
Grant all able
Bodies the
Motivation they
Need,
To go out and
Work, and to be
Spiritual in
Their capabilities
To succeed.

Lord rebuke the
Proud, the lazy,
The drug dealers and
The "too good for work snobs."
For many kids are hungry
Today simply because
Parents refuse to find
A job.

Use the hard workers
In the fields and those
In the factories working
Day and night,
To influence and encourage
That able sister or brother
to stray away from drugs
and prostitution when they
know that it's not right.

God show them
That fast money will never
Last.
Through hard work and
Honesty their struggles
Shall come to past.

Father you said,
Seeking your kingdom
Will allow us to
Be worried free.
However we must,
"Never be lazy,
but work hard
and serve the Lord
enthusiastically"
AMEN

Lord Align My Mind With My Heart

Have you ever looked outside and notice how big the moon was? Have you walked outside and notice how the birds sing and fly no matter what happens in life? Have you ever walked along a lake and admired the beauty of the water, wondering how it compliments the sky, yet it is a world full of congestion and confusion in between the heavens and the water? If ever you have taken the time out to acknowledge nature and appreciate its existence, then surely you are closer to peace than you think. As I am growing in the word and in prayer, I am becoming closer to the holy spirit and all that it has to offer. Sometimes we get so caught up in our tribulations and all the bad news that goes on in the news and in our communities, which all we know how to do is complain and lash out on others. When we fail to see our blessings in the midst of the storm, we are not at peace with ourselves. We are not being obedient to God. For we are suppose to praise him even when we are facing life's most difficult challenges. We must know that he is GOD and he is going to lead us out of the darkness and into the light. God is able. You must plant your heart and soul in the word so that your faith will increase and nothing or no one will be able to question your walk with Jesus Christ. I know sometimes it gets hard, when you look around and reach out for someone to hold on to, but all you find is a cold bed, a dark room and in most cases a judging friend. However, know that God sits high but he looks low. That's why it is important to manifest yourself in the word and continue on in prayer so that you will reap the benefits of the Holy Spirit. Love, Joy, Peace, longsuffering, gentleness, goodness and faith. Many may act or seem like they hold these things because of their monetary status and the people whom they feel makes them feel such things. However, to truly have nothing, to truly be condemned, to truly be judged wrongfully and to struggle long, yet still you feel Joy and Peace because of God's promise, then you are experiencing the Holy Spirit and all that it has to offer. Rejoice today as you know that God will never leave you nor forsake you. Just like an ice cold glass of water in the middle of the desert, there's nothing like having peace of mind, like a good night's sleep in a California king bed with pillow top mattresses overlooking the city lights, after sleeping on a hard mat as a homeless soul outside of the busy streets of Chicago, there's just nothing more comforting than a peace of mind. Pray this prayer for your strength in the Lord as you search for a peace of mind. God is able!

GALATIANS 5:22

"But the fruit of the Spirit is love; joy, peace, longsuffering, gentleness, goodness, faith,"

Dear God,
Please give me comfort in my
heart as it struggles with decisions
deep within.
Calm my soul as I
toss and turn in

the bed I try to sleep in.
As I'm driving down
the street in
this busy life,
give me peace.
Even though the
crime rate is
high and the worries
of financial stability
has increased.
Even in the midst
of my sinful past
I'm dealing with on
today,
Father you said
once you walk
in the holy spirit,
all our sins would
be washed away.
Heavenly father,
you are alpha and omega,
the beginning and the end!
So as I fight with the
devil in my heart,
I know your word
will conquer and win!
Help me to keep a
clean slate when others
challenge my faith.
Help me to replace good
with bad as I
learn to love those
full of hate.
Forgiving
others as well as

myself,
is far more
precious than
a rich man's wealth.
It is only then
I can reap
the benefits of
your fruitful spirit.
As I walk in
your word,
I can feel it and
hear it!
Joy, Peace
faith and Love!
Hear my prayer
 O Father above!
You said we
are promised sorrow
on this earth at
some point and time.
So give me strength
where there is weakness,
but most of all
a peace of mind.
AMEN

One Day At A Time

Have you ever woke up and felt like you just didn't have the energy to get out of bed? You just want to lie down and forget about the problems of the world? Well I've been there. I know how it feels to want to forget about it all. However, you have to dig deep within yourself and know that GOD has a plan for your life and he is working on and preparing a plan for your life. The only way you can receive it is if you stand up, get up and face the world another day! It's easy to give up and just die physically and mentally because of the problems you go through, but it takes strength, power and prayer to stand tall and face the enemy when it seems as if you are loosing. When God is is for you, then who can be against you? When GOD is speaking to you and through you, who can deny the power of the holy spirit? Know God's voice and know when he is speaking to you and reaching out to you because that is where your blessings will come from. When you can't see the road ahead, when you don't know where your next meal is coming from and when the world tells you that you have lost the battle ahead, know that God is real and he is able! Know that GOD had the final say in your life. Your wife, husband, children, parents, boss or best friend can only give you advice, but that is worldly advice. The kind of knowledge and power we get from our Lord goes far beyond human thinking. GOD is of the heaven so his way of thinking is heavenly; man is of earth, so our way of thinking is earthly. Reach for a higher understanding, and only then can you and will you gain the strength and wisdom you need to fight life's difficult race. Pray this prayer for your strength in the Lord as you seek power to make it through this life one more day. Don't give up, GOD is able.

ISAIAH 41:13

"For I am the LORD, your God, who takes hold of your right hand and says to you, Do not fear; I will help you."

Dear God,
Please give me the
Strength to take on
This difficult task.
Help me to climb
This high mountain
Today Lord I ask.

Even when the odds
Are against me
And the darkness
Is great,
Grant me the
Determination I
Need through
Faith.

Put my enemies
Behind me
When they stand

In my way.
Make them
My ladder
Heavenly father
On this day.

There are
Many of your
Children in the
Midst of a struggle
Right now.
Give them the
Tools they need,
Guide them, hold
Them and teach
Them how.

Carry us over
Trouble waters
So that all
Sinners can see,
Anything is
Possible through
Christ Jesus
If we only
Believe.

Father sometimes
I grow weary,
my head hangs
Low and my
Body gets weak.
I don't know
How I will
Make it
Through these
Long hard weeks.

Grant me strength
Today as I continue
To walk in your
Word and stand true.
Heavenly father you said,
"Do not fear;
I will help you."
AMEN

When God Is With You Who Can Be Against You

Have you ever been on a job where it felt like everyone was against you? It seemed like no matter what you did, it was never enough? There were certain people that would get away with murder and there was nothing no one could do about it? I've been there. If you work in the real world long enough you will find yourself in at least one place where there are people who should not be in leadership positions because they look down on their workers and they don't recognize the good that you do. If you find yourself among people who constantly criticize your work and try to put you down because of jealousy and hate, do not fear and do not give up. When you are a child of GOD there will be many situations in your life when people's wicked ways try to hold you back so they can shine and get glory. Jesus assures us that they may plot and plan, yet they may even get away with the first few acts, but Jesus will soon bring the wicked ways to an end. When we fight evil with evil, we make it difficult for Jesus to bless us. Be patient and don't get revenge. Continue doing what you know in your heart is right. If you know your quality of work and your morals are at the level in which you know they should be, then do not fear what will happen on your job. Surely your boss or supervisor may plot against you but no authority is higher Jesus. When others try to bring you down Jesus will wait until the time is right and then he will use your enemy as your foot stool. There were times when I was treated wrongly by people in leadership positions at my job and they were bought to shame in front of the whole office. Jesus has a way of showing you the end result of others mis-using you. So don't take matters into your own hands because the Lord knows that his day his coming. The enemy has a way of making us feel like we have to follow their wicked ways, or we don't have a voice in things in which we know we should, but hold on to your faith because GOD will remove you from that situation. Many times people quit, runaway, or simply just give up hope when they don't see any way out of a bad situation in the workplace. Jesus has a plan. He knows what's going to happen before it happens. He knows how much we can take and he'll never put too much on us. Stand strong and continue to do good. Keep your spirit alive, let your light shine and treat your enemies with respect although they may not respect you. When we hold tight to our pride constantly worried about what others think of us, and then we interfere with God's plan for us. The only way we can fight evil is with good. Don't worry about man rewarding you because when Jesus rewards us it's always more than man could ever give us. When others do me wrong, I'm actually excited because I know that GOD is going to make sure that I get the blessings I deserve. At one point in my life, it seemed as if the more people treated me bad the higher I would climb. Keep the gossip going, keep the lies and the jealousy going because everything you say and do to me is going to come back and haunt you one day. Jesus said he would never leave nor forsake us no matter what. Know that and believe it in your heart so when people try to convict you, Jesus will be right there holding your hand. So many times the media tried and have talked so bad about celebrities that it drove them into a state of depression. Many times they would just want to hide from the world. That's what people will do to you if you allow the things they say and do to you to linger in your heart and mind. We all know our faults and we know when and what we need to change but never let others take away from who you are. Use your GOD given strength because it keeps us grounded. With his word alone our jobs, friends, families and even the media can't bring us down because when GOD is on our side who can be against us. The bible says don't worry because his day is surely coming. Don't just say it, but pray this prayer for strength on your job. God is able!

I'm reminded of a Psalms today, 37: 12-13

"The wicked plots against the just, and gnashes at him with his teeth, the Lord laughs at him, for he sees that his day is coming."

"Cast your burden on the LORD, and He shall sustain you; He shall never permit the righteous to be moved" (Psalm 55:22).

Dear God,

I come to you today to ask that you may grant me the courage to stay strong.

I've been faithful in my walk with you and telling others of your glory for so long.

Right now I am facing one of life's trying challenges that you said I would come upon.

Father you said you would give us power as we can do all things through your son.

Jesus please allow your spirit of righteous to enter my work place each day,

Despite the odds of this world against me, despite what my enemies may say.

I know that it's your power and will that prevails in the end.

Please teach me Lord, today to be patient because I know with prayer the righteous always wins.

You said when there is nothing else left to do, to just stand still in your word,

Even when the plot of evil is so loud in this world, I know my silent cry in faith is heard.

Dear God, please help me to realize that sometimes we must move on despite the past,

Please help me to understand if this job is no longer for me or if it's meant to last.

You see I'm not worried about man and what he may think and do,

Because I know that my guidance and my directions all come from you.

Although I can't see it now, please help me to keep my faith toward the hills,

As this world tries to bring me down, may I forever stay on the right path and do your will.

My enemies surround me, yet with my armor of God there is nothing they can do,

Because you said, "Cast your burdens upon the Lord, and he shall sustain you."

AMEN

Tomorrow Is Not Promised

When I was younger my grandmother used to take my sister and I to many funerals. It was frightening to see those people lying there still. I grew to be fearful of death. I'm sure that is normal for all humans to fear the unknown. When you are not walking in the word of God it is only natural that you will fear death or the end of the world. However, when you read God's word and believe what it written, you can rest assure that you will only die a physical death but your soul will rise to heaven. You will forever be happy and peaceful! You will be among the precious angels and the Father, Son and holy spirit! You will not weep for sadness, only joy; you will feel no pain but love unconditionally. You will not judge others or be judged. You will be among the Saints that God has chosen! When you fear God, then your fear of the world will decrease. When you can live your life each day knowing if your heavenly father calls you at any moment and you will be okay with that, then you are at peace with yourself. You are growing spiritually. My sister's uncle is a famous basketball star that many may know, Joe Dumars. I grew up in the Dumars household. When Joe's father, Joe Dumars Sr. passed away, the famous group THE WINANS sung a song at his funeral. I was young, but I still remember it today. It was called MILLIONS. The chorus went a little like this, "Millions didn't make it, but I was one of the ones who did." Meaning, many lost souls will not make it to heaven, but thank God I was one of the ones who did. That is so powerful! If you know someone today who is struggling with unbelief, give them a word from God. Today we are loosing so many to fatal car accidents, plane crashes, homicide, suicide and sickness. When famous people pass away, it opens our eyes because we know if they are here today and gone tomorrow, we can be as well. Time is winding up and this world will soon be over. Whether death catches up with you before our fathers in heaven comes or not, make a change in your life today. Reach a sinner, help a family member or simply change your selfish ways. God sees all and he hears all. Do not let our good Savior catch you sleeping. There is much work to be done. Pray this prayer for your strength in the Lord as you prepare for a heavenly lifestyle instead of a worldly one. God is able!

MARK 13:36

"If he comes suddenly, do not let him find you sleeping.
What I say to you, I say to everyone: 'Watch!' "

Dear God,
Please forgive me for all my sins,
because I understand if I confess
them today,
your mercy and grace will
bring evil invitations to an end.

Dear God,
I ask for your forgiveness today,
because If not,
I will call and get no answer
but God your son is all I've got!

Dear God,
Your son gave his life,
just so that we might
have everlasting peace.
The more I read
and understand
your word,
my faith, hope
and love
continues
to increase.

Father,
you said no
man knows the day
nor the hour
you will appear.
However, If I
just stay manifested
in your word,
my voice
you will continue
to hear.

Father I know
if we just believe
and receive you
as our King,
Our place in
heaven will be
guaranteed.

But Lord,
I want to make
you proud at
that gate,
never ashamed!
I want you to
say,
"THAT IS
MY CHILD"
and be proud
to call me
by name!

I want you
to look over
my life,
and say,
"My child,
you've done
my will."
The only
way this
will happen
is if I
listen to you
and be still!

When you come
home with all
glory in your
hands,
I want to
live my life
in a way that
you believe
I can.

Whether I'm
helping a friend,
or a family member
in the time of
distress,
Whether I'm
picking up the
phone to call
my child,
or making
someone's
"no" a
"yes".

When you
return father,
I can and will
make you proud.
My prayers
you've answered,
and my blessings
you've delivered
plenty and loud.

When you
return, I will
not be slumbering
or sleeping,
Or focusing on
life's unpredictable
clock,
Because you've
warned us all
and
The word teaches
us,
"What I say to you, I say to everyone:'
Watch"
AMEN

A Doctor In The Sick Room

Sickness and disease play a major role in destroying this nation today. So often we wake up every morning and complain about driving, complain about having to talk to certain people, and how others look at us. Instead of being so negative we need to think God that we have legs to drive, that we can use our tongue to speak and that we have eyes to even see how people look at us. Everyday we wake up with our health and strength is a blessing. Only when we are sick and down, whether it is a cold or maybe a bruised hand, that we can truly appreciate the use of our body, the strength to move and walk. God has favor of you as you walk and talk today. Many are sick today because of various reasons. Just because you have a sickness or disease does not mean the Lord does not love you. Sometimes he takes away our ability to do something so that we can seek him and ask for his mercy and grace. Sometimes his will for us may be something we were not expecting. Maybe through our struggles we may bless others when they see how easy it is to loose your health and strength. Though you may be sick and the doctor says it is impossible, maybe the cure is too expensive, you keep your faith in the Lord and never give up because God healed those who had such strong belief in his power. Believe that he is the final Doctor that will give healing, believe that he is the prescription writer, and he is your strength in the time of pain. Pray this prayer for your strength in the Lord to heal your sickness or those who you know may be sick. God mercy is sufficient and he is able.

LUKE 9:11

"And the people, when they knew it, followed him: and he received them, and spoke unto them of the kingdom of God, and healed them that had need of healing."

Dear God,
    We know you have the power to heal and restore all things great and small.
    Diseases and sickness is slowly contributing to our nation's fall.

    Heavenly father many don't know that you can re-new their pain and sickness.
    Allow your holy spirit to speak in nursing homes and hospitals
    where there is need for deliverance.

    Rebuke Satan as he tries to bring HIV into homes that have fallen short of sin,
    and sexual diseases that are generated between unfaithful women and men.

    I pray that many will turn away from drugs that are making their bodies' deteriate.
    I pray that you give the lame strength to walk again so that their faith can become great.

    I pray that you grant sight to at least one blind man today,

And that someone might hear this prayer and inspire those who are weak to come your way.

Jesus grant us power through prayer to guide doctors as patients go under the knife,
that they might have the knowledge and wisdom to preserve life.

Dear God, those who are having test ran to see if their cancer is deadly right now,
stop the spread and heal them father in your name, someway somehow.

My faith tells me you're able to make all things new and complete.
The same things you did in the past you are still doing as we speak.

For sometimes you give us sickness so that we might pray and see that your miracles are real.
Father I pray that many may look to you when sickness seems impossible to heal.
AMEN.

Thank God For My Wife

Now when I wrote this poem I started thinking of the things that a Christian woman wanted to say so many times, but never have the nerves. So many times we get caught up in life and all that it has to offer. Even when we do the will of God we feel like we don't have time for anything else and sex is the last thing on our mind. If sex is on our mind we may feel as if we are never sexy or pretty enough because the world makes it convenient for the super models and the woman around the corner to be the center of attention. I am here to say that you can be that fire in his eye, you can be that woman on the cover of sports illustrated and you can feel like you are everything he wants and need if you just believe that. A lot of times women don't wear certain clothes because they feel as if they are being disobedient to God. We all have our opinions in life. What may be pretty to one woman or man may be ugly to another, what may be disrespectful to one woman or man may be beautiful to another. You don't have to look like a house maid to be obedient to God, because there might be a man looking at you that likes how house maids look. You will never please man. You have to please yourself and look good for you! When you feel confident around yourself, your husband will feel it and he will lavish in your sexiness. God made Adam and

Eve because he wanted us to embrace each other's sexuality. Shame on those who have evil thoughts and lust for someone else' wife. That is the sin in him. It's not the outfit that she wears. Make your husband proud today. God judges us from the inside and if no one else knows, he knows our intentions. If they are not of him, it will not prosper. Wives, look good for yourself, feel good for yourself and then you will be all that he needs. Take care of your body, keep it clean and honest. A man only receives what we give him. Be that fresh, honest, truthful and faithful woman that he needs so that he may be the kind of man that GOD has called him to be. Pray this prayer for your strength in the Lord as you become more open and intimate with your husband. GOD IS ABLE!

PROVERBS 5:19

"Let her be as the loving hind and pleasant roe; let her breasts satisfy thee at all times; and be thou ravished always with her love."

Oh Precious father in Heaven,
Please continue to
lift my marriage to new heights.
In doing so,
make it so that my
husband
longs for me each
and every night.

May I take care of
my body, because it
belongs to him
and his body's
mine.
Sometimes we

get busy with
kids and work
that love making
on some days,
we may not
have time.

Lord help us
both to make
time to shower each
other with love
and grace.
Although I may
not like parts
of my body,
let him cherish
it with his warm
embrace.

Keep my priority
in pleasing my
husband on the
top of the list.
May the fire
never stop
burning each
time we kiss.

Father we
sometimes allow
anger and frustration
to punish our men
from sexual pleasure.
May we look
deeper into the needs

of a husband
and not allow
our faults to be the
measure.

From time
to time may
I dress up for
him
and feel sexy
even as we grow old.
May our love
inspire other couples
whose marriage
has gone cold.

We know we
are one in you Christ
and our marriage
bonded from heaven
above.
As you said
in your word
may my
"breast satisfy thee
all the time;
and be thou
ravished always
with my love."
AMEN

"And If I Be Lifted Up From This Earth, Will Draw All Men Unto Me"

When things are going well in my life, I often forget to do the things in which I know I need to do to follow God. Such as not reading his word as much, not praying at night and simply not doing his will. Many may look and judge, but it is so easy to get off track. It only takes one day, then two, then a week of disobedience and it throws your life off track. Like you're off balanced and you are about to fall. So is it when we do not follow God on a day to day basis. There will always be trials and tribulations. The devil is just waiting for the moment to be invited into a Christian's home. His word says, "The fear of the LORD tendeth to life: and he that hath it shall abide satisfied; he shall not be visited with evil." (Proverbs 19:23)

We may say, "Oh I didn't invite the devil, I'm not that stupid." Yes we did, when we watch television about bad news, we are welcoming evil into our house, when we are lusting for those things in which we know is not for us, but is good to us, we are inviting evil in our home, when we sit and talk about the sins of others and laugh with our neighbors, we are saying, "Devil come in and have a sit, would you like a drink?" The devil is sneaky, he sneaks his way into our homes so if we don't have the armor of God's protection around us on a day to day basis, then we will be in a war battle with evil. Yes, as Christians we will win, but to avoid the fight, let's be obedient so we don't have to worry about the darkness. Stay in the light. God is our salvation and light, whom shall we fear? Pray this prayer for your strength in the Lord as you learn to follow him more abundantly. God is able.

PROTECT US TODAY HEAVENLY FATHER AS WE STRIVE TO FIND OUR WAY.
LEAD US DOWN THE PATH IN WHICH YOU HAVE SET FOR EACH OF US TODAY.

FOR WE KNOW THAT YOU HAVE A PLAN FOR ALL OF US IN DUE TIME,
BUT HELP ME TO REALIZE THAT YOUR WILL IS MORE IMPORTANT
THAN THIS WILL OF MINE.

HELP ME TO HAVE PATIENCE WHEN OTHERS JUDGE ME SO.
TEACH US LORD THE POWER OF FAITH AND WHAT WE NEED IN ORDER
THAT IT GROWS.

SHOW OTHERS AND MYSELF THAT LOVING EACH OTHER IS LIKE LOVING
YOU.
AND TEACH US TO FORGIVE OUR BROTHERS AND SISTERS NO MATTER
WHAT IT IS THAT THEY MAY DO.

JESUS WE KNOW THAT YOU DON'T ASK OF US, ANYTHING THAT YOU

DIDN'T DO ON YOUR OWN.

YOU LOVE AND FORGIVE US ALL THE TIME, EVEN WHEN WE KNOW WE'VE DONE WRONG!

JESUS YOU SAID THAT YOU ARE THE TRUTH AND THE LIGHT AND NO

ONE COMES TO THE FATHER BUT THROUGH YOU,

LEAD US INTO YOUR LIGHT CHRIST SO THAT OUR HEARTS MAY NEVER

DOUBT THAT YOUR WORD IS TRUE.

FOR TODAY JESUS THERE ARE MANY TRAILS AND TRIBULATIONS THAT

WE FACE.

YOU SAID THAT THESE THINGS SHALL HAPPEN BEFORE YOU ARRIVE

FROM THAT HEAVENLY PLACE.

THE HURRICANES, DISEASES AND NATIONS RISING UP AGAINST ONE

ANOTHER.

FALSE PROPHETS GUIDING OUR CHILDREN AND SISTERS AND BROTHERS

TURNING THEIR BACKS ON ONE ANOTHER.

THE EARTHQUAKES, THE TALK OF WAR EVEN THE SEASONS ARE HARD

TO DISTINGUISH RIGHT NOW.

WE KNOW IT'S YOUR VOICE THAT ROARS THROUGH THESE CLOUDS TRYING

TO GET OUR ATTENTION SOME HOW.

ONLY FEW LISTEN, AND ONLY FEW KNOW OF YOUR GLORY TODAY.

PLEASE GIVE ME THE POWER TO BRING AT LEAST ONE SOUL YOUR WAY.

HELP US O HOLY ONE TO LOOK BY FAITH, THE THINGS IN WHICH HUMAN EYES CAN'T SEE,

BECAUSE YOU SAID, "AND IF I BE LIFTED UP FROM THIS EARTH, WILL DRAW ALL MEN UNTO ME."

AMEN.

As For Me And My House

Although we all walk our different paths in life when it comes to the Lord, the teaching starts at home. The example starts at home, and the peace starts at home. Home should be our comfort, our place where we lay our burdens. Where we can be free. If you have a hostile environment or a relationship with someone in your house that is not of GOD and separate from the lifestyle that you are living, then it is not right. God wants us to embrace one another, share with one another in our home the things in which are hindering us in our life. When you walk outside, there is a world out there waiting to eat you alive. If you don't have that support at home, then you will be tossed and driven, but you will be alone. There's nothing like having someone on your side that supports and love you. God said, "Where two or three are gathered in my name, there I would be also." So often we try to help the neighbor, co-worker, church member or friend, but all alone our family at home needs a warm hug, a word of inspiration and the courage to make it another day. Yes we should reach out all across God's land, but if we can't make our home a place of God, when those who visit us come into a hostile environment, then our giving is in vain. You never know when Jesus may show up at your door. Let your light shine in your home and accept no evil doers to display their works in your house. Tell them like the old folks used to say, "You ain't gotta go home, but you gotta get HELL out of here!" Pray this prayer for your strength in the Lord as you continue or start building a home that will be known as a house of God. God is Able!

JOSHUA 24:15

"But as for me and my house,
we will serve the lord."

Dear God,
    I will not allow evil to come in and destroy my home.
    At all times I will keep the bible open in my house because I know I can't do it alone.

    Seeking your guidance will help me to create a holy atmosphere,
    and give me the power to rebuke Satan whenever he appears.

    Dear God, if a stranger comes to my door in need of anything,
    I will gladly give him a place to rest and comfort in your name.

    I will not turn away the handicap or the poor, because we never know who you may use to bring blessings to our door.

    I pray that my own family will keep your word close to their heart,
    So when others try to break our bond, nothing will keep us apart.

And as my child goes to school everyday, please keep him on the right track,

so that he may immediately fall on his knees when the enemy tries to attack.

Father you have given us everything we need to live,

Such as Faith, prayer and your only begotten son so that our sins you might forgive.

All that you ask is that we may glorify you.

I don't know about others, but Father, that's just what I'll do.

Each day it is a struggle out here, and times continue to get hard,

"But as for me and my house, we will serve the Lord."

AMEN

Be Not Unequally Yoked

Relationships are one of the biggest challenges that we face in this life. So often we get caught up in mankind and all that they can provide for us physically and mentally that we fail to glorify God. The one who provides us the opportunity to even spend social time with one another. Many of us find Christ Jesus through the trials and tribulations of our relationships with our lovers. However, when we are spending so much time and energy in trying to make a man or woman into the person that we want them to be, and when we spend so much time trying to pull them into the word and Christ, (yet they reject your offer), it eventually takes its toll on you as a person. My pastor once preached a sermon of how God wants us to reach into the darkness and bring others into the light. However many of us get that confused. God doesn't want us to actually walk in the darkness, just reach out. Sometimes helping others just isn't enough and it causes us to stumble. Reach the sinners, but don't become like them. We have to know when something or someone is not for us. Love is true and it is unselfish. Love is not blind. You have to know when someone is looking out for your best interest. If a person doesn't care about the good of themselves, then how can they be concerned about you? Without God we will be tossed and driven.   A man or woman who chooses to make decisions without God in their life are lost souls.   If you are living this lie with them, you will reap the ungodly benefits that they bring upon themselves.   You can't change anyone; they have to want to change on their own.   That's why we have prayer.   The power of prayer is wonderful.   Pray for them everyday.   Yet do not allow their problems to consume you.   God has a will and a plan for us all.   Pray this prayer for your strength in the lord as you struggle in your relationships with others today.   God is able and he is God all by himself!

2 CORINTHIANS 6:14

"Do not be unequally yoked together with unbelievers.
For what fellowship has righteousness with lawlessness?
And what communion has light with darkness?"

Dear God,
I pray for my sisters and brothers today
looking for love.
So often do we follow our own will
Instead of our heavenly father's above.

I pray today dear Father,
for the sister that is laying
with an unbelieving man.
The sister who wants to
change him and really
thinks she can.

He tells her that he
doesn't have to believe
what she believes in.
However, father you know
an unbeliever will

quickly bring
her close to death
and sin.

I pray for that brother
today, who is in love
with a woman who
doesn't believe.
For she is seductive
and always have
tricks up her sleeve.

Father I pray for
these sisters and
brothers looking
to find love in
all the wrong places.
Yet they read your
word and pray,
but will allow
their weakening hearts
and strong minds to
trade places.

Father touch the
spirit of those
Contemplating
on getting married
or engaged.
Help them to see
that sometimes
it does matter
the experiences
and the age.

Sometimes it takes
others a while to come
to you God.
So they may be
holding back the
blessings of others
who are doing your will Lord.

However, Father God
we know that you want
all believers to reach
out to those who
don't know you,
everyday.
So it is our job to
tell them about your
mercy through our
spiritual ways.

Yet when we
are choosing a
partner to serve
you in this life,
Father it is
your will that
we both are
spiritual bound,
husbands and wives.

Dear God,
help this world to see,
if you have to wonder
or carry the load for
your lover,
If you have to pray
alone,
and can't praise
God with each other,

Please re-think your decision
today before your spirit goes broke.
For your word clearly states God,
"Be not unequally yoked."
AMEN.

"Be Still And Know That I Am God"

There were many times in my life where I tried to fight battles that were just too big for me to fight. If I was unhappy with my friends or love one's actions, I would try to convince them to change. I would try to change them into the person in which I felt that they should be. It would only blow up in my face and cause a distance between us. I soon realized that this was God's department. Some things are just too much for us to handle. We have to sit back and allow GOD to work in people's life. Many times I want to save the world. As I said before, I love people. I have friends of different cultures and attitudes. Some were nice, mean, happy, funny, sad, impatient, or maybe just weird. Yet they all have a distinctiveness that can be appreciated. At times I would try to get everyone together so we could have a good time but it would never work out quite like I planned. Everyone was too different and someone would not like the other. I could never understand because I've always been the type of person to get along with people. I would try to play the middle man between those not getting along, trying to bring them together. It would cause a burden upon me because I would be caught in the middle. I think sometimes GOD shows me that there is a time and place for certain things and certain people. Often we try to do things that are meant for GOD and he wants us to "be still" meaning stop trying to do his job and let him worry about things that are out of our jurisdiction. There are certain things that we can change and control but the power of GOD goes far beyond what we can even dream of doing. I learned to have more faith and allow Jesus to do his work. So often we look to other people and things for help when all along he is standing by just waiting for us to call his name. "Know that I am GOD". Jesus has done so much for this world that we should automatically know to fall on our knees and allow his glory to shine down on situations that we can't control.

I can recall when I was working in Atlanta Georgia. I was so busy working, going out and just having fun until I allowed my priority with GOD to go astray. I wasn't going to church on Sundays because I didn't have time. I was too tired after all the busy activities in my life. I stopped praying at night because I just didn't have time. Well one day I fell on hard times and it seemed as if no one was around to help me. I felt helpless and lonely. I couldn't understand why GOD was allowing this to happen to me. I looked up to the sky and asked GOD, "Why is this happening to me? Why didn't you help me out of this situation?" Then a strange feeling came over me. I knew GOD was speaking to my heart in his own way saying, "Because you didn't ask my child. Ask and you shall receive, seek and you shall find, knock and the door shall be open." I then realized that this whole time all I had to do was just turned to Jesus, he was there waiting on me to come to him. From then on I always made a vow to take time out for GOD. If it's no more than going to the bathroom at work or pray on my way to work. Making it a habit to keep the lines of communication open between myself and Jesus made life so much easier. We would be surprised the power of faith and just asking GOD to be there for us throughout the day. How quickly do we look for people of high authority and high profile jobs to put in a good word for us, when all along Jesus is there waiting on us to put in a good word for ourselves. Take time out today from the busy world. Listen to GOD as he speaks through nature, through the chirping of the birds or simply the leaves falling on the trees; informing us that the seasons are changing and there's new work to be done but don't forget to pray. For he said, " Be still and know that I am GOD." Pray this prayer to God for your strength in simply being still. God is able.

PSALMS 46:10

"Be still and know that I am GOD"

Dear God,
Please help me to resist
Fighting the enemy on my own.
Lead me in the right direction when
I stray away from your word alone.

Teach me be to be good
To my neighbor,
In the mist of hate.
Teach me to stand on faith
When my worries are great.

Often times we break down
When the troubles of life appear.
Our hearts begin to fear,
But your word states so clear,

If you could feed the birds of
The air everyday,
Surely we should trust,
How much more would
The Heavenly father feed us.

Dear God, help me
To recognize your voice from near and afar.
Although I may be surrounded by
The enemy,
I know Where ever I am,
There also
You are.

When the odds are against me,
And the road seems dangerous
A head.
Remind me of your grace
And mercy so that I may
Grow courageous when scared.

So it may be, when
The storm clouds of war
Begin to roar
And my actions lead me
 In
Times that are hard.
I eventually will,
"Be still and know that you are GOD.
AMEN

Change My Heart O Lord

Have you ever met someone that just seem like they were just too good to be true? Their lives were just too perfect and they did everything according to life's rules? Well nine times out of ten, the truth would eventually come out. No one is living the life of a fairy princess or prince. Life is full of trials and tribulations and if someone tells you that its not, then their intentions are false. I've learned that many times, people who are crying out for help try to cover up the guilt and sin they are committing in order to live a lie through you. Don't allow someone else' burden to play a part in your life. Be watchful and alert because the devil will tell you that if you just choose to follow this person or belief that things will be better for you when only it leads to destruction and deceit. Many times we fall into this trap by allowing messed up relationships to emotionally take us over. For example, I truly thought this guy was the one for me because he was everything that my man wasn't. I mean he knew what to do and how to do it. It seemed as if he was heaven sent. I was soon to learn that he was not as perfect as the man I was about to leave him for. Ever heard the term, "the grass is not always greener"? The devil knows how to really do it. He will have you thinking that the sins you are committing are really what you need in your life. As time went on I realized that the things in which GOD had in place for me were not things or people I needed to hide from the world. There's no way that he was going to send me someone else' husband. When he sent me a man, it was going to be my own. When he sends a blessing, it's not in disguise. For we will know by the fruit it bears. If something doesn't sit right with you in your heart and mind, if there is something about someone that you just can't put your finger on, you need to research. You need to look deeper. GOD speaks to us in our dreams, in signs and he also speaks to us through other people. If we just close our mouths long enough sometimes to hear the Holy Spirit speaking then we will be able to see the things in which GOD is trying to show us. Additionally, when a person is filled with the Holy Spirit everything around them shines. If someone is around you and their light isn't shining so bright, then maybe something in them is not right. Don't just say it, but pray this prayer for God to change your heart so you will be able to recognize his voice. God is good!

MARK 7:8

"You have let go of the commands of God And are holding on to the traditions of men."

Dear Heavenly father,
Please help me to
realize that
As I renew my
Spirit today,
There are things
I have to let go
Of in order
To serve you the
Right way.

So Often do we
Fall victim
To man's
Way of doing things.
We separate ourselves
From you father
And the blessings
That you want to
Bring.

Father,
Teach me today,
How to see the
Difference
Between a lavish
House, and a
Christian home.
Many times we
Fool ourselves
In thinking
We are Godly
And nothing is
Wrong.

I know I have
To bury myself in
Your word,
So that I won't
Drown in the
Traditions of men.
When we give our
Lives to you God,
We gain understanding
By being born again.

I know
I don't have all
The answers Dear God.
You said some things
We will never understand.
What's easy to
You, to mankind seem hard.

Father in your word
You said,
We are earthly,
So our way of
Thinking is so,
But you are
Heavenly and
Your way of
Thinking is on
A level that we
In this life,
Will never know!

Thank you for
Your mercy and grace.
Help me to change my
Earthly ways in
Order to fight
The trials I
Face.

Help me to show
Others that everything
We do,
Isn't always right.
Let your holy spirit
Reign on me so
That my wisdom
May climb to new
Heights.

Reveal to me
Oh holy one,
Those things that
Hinder my walk with you.
May I gain strength and
Understanding in the
Word as I serve you.

When I stand at
Those heavenly gates,
I will not bring you
Shame as I come in!
I will not hear
You say,
"You have let go of
The commands of God
And are holding on to
The traditions of men."
AMEN

Father I Stretch My Hands To Thee

Have you ever tried to clean a spot on your carpet and it didn't work? Have you ever just scrubbed and scrubbed? You went to the store and you purchased all these carpet cleansing material, even rented a carpet cleaner vacuum? Well I have. You keep trying to do things the cheap way, and you keep trying to do things on your own. You know good and well you need to hire a professional carpet cleaner because they will come in and get that spot clean immediately! Finally, you see that this is the only way your carpet is going to be cleaned and new. So you call them up. The same applies to our lives with Christ. We go through things in our life that stains our spirit and heart. We think we can make it if we have certain people or materialistic things that will help us to forget about the pain. Whether it is drugs, money, sex or people that we meet. These things can never compare to the love of our Lord and Savior. As much as we try to go throughout this life and handle our own problems, we will not prosper. You can only go so far without Jesus. I was talking to my Aunt Vicki today and she said, "Baby, I just don't see how people make it through life without God." That was so true. You can only go so far. There comes a time in your life when you have to get on your knees and call upon the Lord! Momma may be mother, papa may be father, but they can't deliver you from your past and your burdens like Christ can. He can cleanse your soul and make you new and whole. He can wipe away your tears and your fears. Each day is a new day and another chance to make things right with the Lord. Pray this prayer for your strength in the Lord as you reach out to the only source that can save you. God is God all by himself. God is able!

Father I stretch my hands to thee, no other source I know.

For you said, just ask and surely you can make the storms go.

For you said, "Seek first the kingdom of God and all things shall be added unto you."

I rest my burdens at the alter knowing that your blessings will

Follow through.

You see man will talk behind my back, lie, cheat and steal,

Not knowing that the wages of sin is death, not knowing that

Your love is pure and real.

I come to you to confess today, Father I stretch my hands to thee.

Right now God please put your armor of protection around me.

Father you said, "Whatever things you ask in prayer, believe and you shall receive."

Speak to me with your holy spirit through others and also in my dreams.

Teach me your way O Lord so that I may touch others.
Jesus grant us the strength we need so that we may be good fathers and mothers.

Father Bless the schools that try to lock you out,
Courthouses and on the jobs. Forgive them for they know not what your
Salvation is all about.

I need you now Lord, Father I stretch my hands to thee.
For your said where 2 or 3 are gathered in your name, so should you be.

So use me as a testimony to tell others of your grace,
And give me the shoes I need to run this difficult race.

For sometimes I stumble Lord, and my faith it grows small.
Help me to increase it and move mountains wide and tall.

For you said if I say to this mountain be removed and cast into the sea, it will be done.
Keep me on the cross father so that I may be a blessing to someone.

Father teach me the essence of patience so that I may stand still as you move in my life.
Father touch lives right now in nursing homes and those in pain and strife.

Allow your holy spirit to reign down on them in comfort and peace,

Because your ways are not ours lord, so surely these days will decrease.

However, your blessings and eternal love never stops giving. It reaches high and high.

So shall I suffer now because you said I'll understand it better by and by.

Father I stretch my hands to thee, please help me to renew my heart.

Make my spirit clean so that I may have a clean slate and a new start.

Please teach us how to let go and how to forgive.

For you said if we do so, a longer and a better life we'll live.

Father you also said your days will be short if you disrespect mother and father.

Please teach our kids this today, and the importance of loving one another.

Father help us to remember that we walk by Faith, and what that really means.

"The substance of all things hoped for and the evidence of things not seen."

Father help us to realize you have a purpose for each and every one of us.

You know our thoughts when we think them; you know our hearts when we fuss.

You know the number of hairs on our heads, our deepest fears and what
Makes us shame,
For you said, "And I call you by name!"

Father I stretch my hands to thee, so that I may not only talk the talk but walk the walk too.

You said let your light shine so bright before men that they may see our good work and glorify you.

For your strength I reach high and I kneel low.

Father I stretch my hands to thee, no other source I know.

Amen

The Power Of Fellowship

Sometimes people don't love themselves enough to seek Jesus and all his righteousness. I've met people in my life that were abused as a child and they feel as if the world is a cruel place and that their life is not worthy of living. How often people commit suicide because they didn't have anyone in their lives to talk to and tell them of the glory and grace of GOD. I've always been one to be careful of the words that grace my tongue. You never know when the things in which you may say or do can affect the life of someone else. Often I talk and joke and even try to persuade someone to believe in what I believe in. At times, they may not ultimately follow my beliefs or automatically come to Christ, but it's been times where there was something I said that triggered a light in someone's life. When you look at people on the street, smile. There could be something in that smile that shows them that life is worth living for one more minute. When you are at the store and that old lady drops a penny, pick it up and rub her arm, it could be something in your touch that she hadn't felt in a while that makes her feel like she has lived a GOD fulfilling life. You never know what's on someone's mind, or what kind of tragedy that they have faced moments before they come in contact with you, so be of good faith and show them that life continues and that people are different and that they can still smile. Jesus will have you in the strangest of places preaching the gospel. Back in the days, there were times when I was in the club and found myself talking to someone with a damaged heart and giving them hope in their relationships. Often times we think we need to let go of people in our lives because of the things in which they are taking us through, but sometimes we have to work for what's for us. Sometimes we have to go through something so we can appreciate what we have. I found myself being that person who helps others realize that they need to hang in there and hold on with faith. GOD is talking to us in an up to date spiritual way. If our youth are in the clubs, go to the clubs and preach the gospel, if they are at the park, go to the park and speak in a playful way, if they are at school or even work, go to the campus and go to the job and speak in a language that they will understand. Sometimes we have to go out and get involved in their world to reach out to them. Church is good and it is my reference to heaven, but the work and the teachings are in the streets and in our schools. My church is my shelter but we still have many others in the storm that need guidance to the church. Don't just say it, but pray this prayer for fellowship in your life and in the life of others. God is good.

PROVERBS 27:17

"As iron sharpens iron, so a friend sharpens a friend"

Dear God,
I know that we are promised
Dark days on this earth.
However father,
Keep me around Godly
People
So that we may

See each other's worth.

When my spouse
And I can't
See eye to eye.
Put us around
Friends who
Will help
Us try.

May our kids
Be surrounded with
Godly people
When we are apart.
May they carry
With them
The armor of
God in their heart.

Dear God,
Help me to be
A blessing to
Others I come in
Contact with
Each day.
At work, in the
Supermarket,
In church and
In every possible
Way.

For sometimes we
Can help others
By a simple word
Of inspiration.
Some may turn
Away from life's
Loud and noisy
Temptation.

Heavenly father,
There are many among
Us, ready to see
Us fail.
I pray for their
Salvation as well.

Father we know,
Being in the presence
Of a Christian,
Brings love,
Patience and
Discipline.

May our family members
See the goodness that
We do,
In hopes that it will
Rub off on their
Lives too.

Thank you Jesus
For placing me
Around Godly
Women and men.
You said in your

Word,
"As iron sharpens iron,
so a friend sharpens a friend."
AMEN

Forgiving Others

It's funny how when you're younger, you don't tolerate people treating you wrong. Cheating when I was in high school meant you must break up with that person. No one wants to be embarrassed and when you are young your pride is mighty and strong. I remember being in a relationship that was fairly good but as soon as I found out my boyfriend cheated, he was history. I was selfish. I wanted to look good to myself and the world and I felt as if I was the perfect girl, so why would anyone cheat on me? Most of the time when we are young we think we are invincible and no one knows as much as we do. We don't pay attention to our flaws because as far as we're concerned, we don't have any! As I experienced life as the years went on, I started to realize that if I keep going through the same things over and over again, and meeting the same people who treat me the same way, then there has got to be something inside of me that I need to change. Imagine that! If you take a closer look and try to find out why people treat you the way they do, you will find out that it could be simply something you are doing, that causes them to react a certain way. Cheating, hitting, cursing and mis-using others is never the way out, but we are all human and we do things that we are not so proud of sometimes. No one is perfect. If we were all perfect and meant to be alike, GOD would not have made us different. Family and friends will let you down sometimes, but you learn to forgive them because it may be a time in your life when you are going to need that person. You take the good with the bad. Don't dwell on the bad things people do, but take the good and use that to keep the positive in your life. A famous person once said, "If you dwell on the bad things people do, you won't be around for the good times." Had I known what I know now, years ago, I would have kept more people around in my life. Surely we all have fallen short of sin and GOD continues to forgive us, time and time again. No matter how I fail, or how I stumble I can surely say that there is a greater power that continues to see the good in me and that is Jesus Christ. How can we possibly expect him to forgive us when we can't forgive each other? He also said "Love others as I have loved you, and this is the greatest gift you can give." I've always told my friends that the things in which they are experiencing and going through, someone else is going through the same thing or even worse. Life comes at us on different levels, in different ways, but we must stand strong and sometimes being strong means forgiving others. For surely, there has come a time or will come a time when you need someone to forgive you. As I talk to old married couples and ask them the secret of how they stay together so long, they always say, "forgiving each other". Life is too short and holding on to negative attitudes and grudges will cut your blessings. A lot of time, forgiving others really means we need to forgive ourselves. I've seen so many situations where people blame others for the way that their life has turned out. We all walk our own path in life and we have a choice to change and turn things around. Sometimes it's just easier to point the finger at someone else because when we look at ourselves and see pain, it hurts. It hurts worse because we have no one to blame but ourselves. So many people are in the state of denial and will never be able to move forward because they are constantly looking for someone else to blame. Truthfully, the answer is deep within. Pray this prayer for your strength in forgiving others. God is able.

LUKE 23:34

*"Then said Jesus, Father forgive them; for they know
not what they do."*

Dear God,
    In the midst of my pain please help me to forgive,
    When my enemies brag about the sinful life they live.

    Help me to treat them with love and kindness,
    And by prayer may you deliver them from their worldly blindness.

    Although they delight in my struggle and heartache,
    Laugh behind my back and constantly remind me of my mistakes.

    Give me the strength to keep anger out of my heart,
    And once I forgive my brother grant him a clean slate and new start.

    Father our earthly ways makes it difficult to do right by the enemy,
    But I know in your Kingdom it will make more sense to me.

    Its funny how man look at power as winning when others loose,
    But the kind of power you speak of is faithful and true.

    It's the kind of power that allows salvation for all.

The kind that will never leave me nor forsake me when I call.

Help me God to deny myself for other's sake, so that I may glorify you
As Jesus once said, "Father please forgive them, for they know
Not what they do."
AMEN

Give Honor To Mother and Father

"Honor your father and your mother, so that you may live long in the land the LORD your God is giving you".

One day when I was going to the flea market in Atlanta Georgia, I saw an old man in the parking lot. He looked as if he was an alcoholic. His clothes wore torn and he looked as if he was drunk. He was talking to a young lady who looked as if she were in her middle 20's. I remember passing him and he said, "Girl you show is looking good today!" I laughed, but at the same time I still spoke to him and I told him thank you. My mom raised me to treat everyone equally. She always told me you never know who or where your blessings will come from. However, as I was getting in my truck to drive off, I heard him tell the young lady, "When you wake up in the morning you pray, you tell the lord to help you go through your day the best way you know how, and you tell him to forgive you for your sins. I am your father and I know I don't always tell you or do the right thing, but you take with you the things you can, and what you can't use, you disregard. I know I'm your father, but I'm not always right." When he said that, something triggered in my heart. So often we look to parents as role models and people who are perfect. Truthfully, parents are just older versions of us. We make mistakes, we are not perfect. We can't possibly depend on parents to lead and guide us down the exact path that we should go. We are all God's children and what works for mom and dad may not work for us. When we depend on our parents to do everything as we think they should, we see failure. Many kids blame their parents for the things in which they go through. Parents are suppose to be loving and they are suppose to give you the basic Morales and values in life so that you can go out in the world and make your own decisions. We are all of man. The bible says, Proverbs 3:5-6 (King James Version)

"Trust in the LORD with all thine heart; and lean not unto thine own understanding.

In all thy ways acknowledge him, and he shall direct thy paths." Trust in the Lord, not mankind. Recently we lost the KING OF POP MICHAEL JACKSON. It was a shock to many, we can't believe it. Imagine how his family feels. For so many years people have talked about his father. How mentally abusive he was to the kids and how they never had an active childhood. No one acknowledge the fact that he worked hard and he believed in his kids enough, that they became successful. Had it not been for their father, we would not be blessed with the musical talent of Michael and the other Jacksons'. The media and this world are quick to point out the bad things. This man gave up a lot for his kids. Michael, Janet and the others would not be who they were to the music industry if it was not for their father. We all have our cross to bare. Mr. Joe Jackson may have had his weaknesses like all of us, but how much better are we than he? The spirit of God makes us all equal and whole. In the great words of Pastor Brown, "That's good news!" When are we going to stop judging one another? We all can do things through Christ who strengthens us.

Disrespecting them and disobeying parents because you don't agree with the decisions they make is wrong and will cause your days to be short. Forgive your parents if they let you down; help them if they have a problem. If parents tell you things in which you feel are wrong, you just disregard those things. Parents gave us life, and for that alone we should be grateful to them and humble ourselves to them like we should with GOD. Like the old man said that day, take what you can use from your parents and move on. When we hate our parents for their decisions and when we don't forgive them, we are making life difficult. GOD gave us parents for a reason. If you drive your parents away for whatever the reason it may be, you will need them one day. Life is hard. Problems and situations occur so often and if we don't have GOD and our parents on our side it can be a long road. The devil knows what makes us mad with our parents and he will use that against us to cut them out of our life. I know that I'm not perfect and that one day my son will disagree with something I do, but I pray to GOD that I bring him up in a way that he will still respect and obey my decisions just because I am his mother. A child is a parents' joy and pride. How they view us means the world to us. If you talk down to your parents it hurts them and it causes a lifetime of pain for you. It will come back on you through your very own children. You will have bad luck and wonder where it came from. There were times when I looked at my siblings and how they treat my mom and it startled me. It startled me because I knew the consequences they would suffer. I'm here today to say, it's not too late to make things right with your parents. It doesn't matter what the situation is or how long it's been damaged because Jesus has a way of healing and

renewing things within us, we didn't know was there. If you ever wonder why some people's life end up worse than others, sometimes it may be how they treated their parents. This evil word has so many strikes against us and if we can do any thing to help create a happier life then we need to do so. Parents are truly not super heroes but they gave us life by way of Jesus who wants us to have it more abundantly. Humble yourself and have patience. When you cut off your parents, you are only hurting yourself. For they are not perfect and they are human. Don't just say it, but pray this prayer for power to respect your parents and elders. God is able!

Leviticus 19:3

"Let every man give honor to his mother and to his father and keep my Sabbaths: I am the Lord your God."

Dear God,
Speak to the youth who have
No limit or control today.
Help the parents to teach
Them to be humble in every way.

Reveal yourself to them and
Teach them your word to stand on.
Show them how to respect
Their elders, even
If he/she is wrong.

For many times our
Parents and elders have
Experiences to share,
Yet sometimes the children
React in mischief and
As if they just do not care.

However, teach these children
To be obedient in their parents eyes.
For an older experienced man

Grows to become very wise.

Teach them to just listen,
As these words of advice
Can help along the way.
Whether following the advice
Of elders or not, at least
Hear what they have to say.

For you said in your word God,
A disobedient child's days
On this earth will be short.
Even if their parents are wrong,
Teach them to be respectful,
So at least
They've done their part.

Father we all know that life's
Challenges will cause
Our
 Patience to go,
However, with your love
And guidance,
The reflection of
Your obedience will
Humble our hearts
And in us,
Honor will grow.

Dear God,
In regards to
Mothers and fathers
Help
The youth to make better decisions.
Let them, Honor parents,

And the elders who surround
Them with "much needed" wisdom.
AMEN

How Excellent

Have you ever been down an old dirt road and you were lost? Your phone didn't have reception? There was no one in the car with you? You knew you had to get home and you didn't have directions at the time. The only way you were going to find your way home was in your own mind. You had to tell yourself, "I will make it home, I have to find a way. I know if I make a right turn it would bring me back here, so I just have to back track." Sometimes God isolates us from certain situations so that we have no other choice but to look deep within ourselves, and no one else for the answers. So the same is for our mental struggles. Sometimes we may feel like no one is there for us or understands what we go through, but if you put your faith in God he will encourage you by being positive and believing in yourself. Know that God will be there for you when it seems impossible. Glorify him when it gets rough, glorify him when it seems like you can't make it because you know that God is good. There is nothing he can't do when faith is involved. When your friends tell you that you will never make it like this, or that you can never succeed doing what you are doing, you tell them that God is a good God and there is no limit to what he can do! That is good news saints. As we go through our trials, it reminds us of how perfect and joyful this love is that God continues to show us. We ought to stand up in the midst of our storm and glorify him and praise his name because he is the GREAT I AM, he is excellent! If you don't know that for yourself then no one else is going to promote that when you are down and out. Be encouraged today, encourage yourself in the word and know that because he is perfect, he is peace, joy and love, he is working things out in your life today. How excellent the GOD is that we serve. Pray this prayer for speaking victory and claiming happiness in your life today. GOD is able.

Psalms 8: 1

"O Lord our Lord, how Excellent is thy
name in all the earth!"

Dear God,
How powerful your name is as it
Grace my tongue.
I want to scream and shout it
As I tell everyone!
When I think about your goodness
And mercy I want to say Jesus
Christ!
How you died for our sins
And gave your life to pay
The ultimate price!
Lord God our Father
In Heaven I want to sing your
Name all the day long,
Because I know when
I speak of your perfection
Nothing can go wrong.
A magnificent word,
A name of power and

Love unconditionally!
I can call on you in the
Time of need and by
Your name you will
Save me!
I can shout Lord Have
Mercy on my life today,
And you will instantly hear
My voice and wipe my sins
Away,
Oh Lord how Excellent
Is thy name!
It brings tears to my
Eyes to sing it
As your word
Brings the devil to shame!
There is no other like it,
And that is good news.
Father I will speak
About the goodness of
Your name in everything I do.
Oh sweet Jesus, with
Arms wide open and
Knees bent,
My heart and my lips declare the same,
Jesus, how excellent is thy name!
AMEN

I Want To Know What Love Is

As I traveled the country during my military career, my relationships with men were not too good. I finally was at a point in my life as to where I didn't need a man because they could not feel a void inside of me. I couldn't understand why I couldn't find this thing called love. Often times I thought I had found it, but I had to learn that Love is not angry, and it is not physically or mentally abusive. I begin to go to church and read my bible. When I was younger, I read my bible because I thought it was just the right thing to do. This time, I wanted to learn more about the word. I wanted to know more about walking with Jesus and having Faith. I prayed and ask GOD to help me understand what I was reading. Surely I found out that "Faith comes by hearing and hearing by the word of GOD". There is truly power in the word because the more I read, the stronger I got and the less I needed anything earthly. I finally felt a joy within myself and didn't need anything or anyone to fill that. I begin to move mountains, all by myself. When GOD has something for you, there is no denying it. I found someone who brings out the best in me. Someone who makes me shine and someone who accepts me for everything

I am, good and bad. Someone who needed me in his life, someone who I can grow with spiritually and physically. I thank GOD for Byron Brown today as I continue my walk with Jesus. We have our ups and downs, and we both have our individual trials and tribulations as we are promised those days on this earth, but surely I have learned and continue to learn from my mistakes. I've learned from my past relationships that you have to appreciate each other; you have to learn to forgive one another because we are all human. You have to have faith and you have to trust one another but most importantly you have to know how to pray together and you have to know what love is. When I was reading the bible and learning what love was, one definition stated, "Love is not selfish" I was selfish back in my younger days. I know that when we are young, we think and act as children, but as we grow we put away those childish ways. Pray this prayer for your strength in the Lord as you understand how God uses others to love us and how his love will fulfill you in a way that this world will never. God is able.

Corinthians 13: 4-5

"Love suffers long and is kind; love does not envy;
love does not parade itself, is not puffed up; 5 does not
behave rudely, does not seek its own, is not provoked,
thinks no evil"

Dear God,
Please help me to keep a loving and
Kind heart.
Show me how to be a good mother
And wife from the very start.

Dear God,
I know that when we

Endure much pain,
Although it hurts,
You'll deposit that
Love back into my
Heart again.

Father, give me the
Strength to put others
Before myself
When I know I should.
Help me to love my
Enemies the way
You told me in
Your word that
I could.

Father in this
World earthly
Goods causes
The heart to stray.
Help me to
Never forget
That your love
And peace can't
Replace that
Any day.

Dear God,
When people see
Me coming, I want
Them to smile.
I want them
To know I am love,
And I am your
Child.

Let the words that
Grace my tongue,
Be acceptable in
Your sight, and
Enlighten everyone.

Dear God,
In this life,
Many believe that
Love is taking and
Not giving,
Many believe love
Is conditional
And sexual living.

Many believe love
Is a one way street
And that it takes
Time to grow.
Dear God,
Your word
Is love and so
Many do not know.

I pray today
For myself and
My sisters and brothers.
Teach us how to be
Patient, giving and
Unconditionally love
One another.

We know in your
Glory, our lights
Will shine so
Bright.
It will lead us out
Of the darkness
And into the light.

Thank you for your
Mercy that some of
Us hold, and in prayer
Others will someday
Find.
In your word you
Said,
"Love suffers long
And is
Kind."
AMEN

Knowing When To Walk Away

From the beginning of our lives we look to our parents for guidance and direction. We look to our parents for love and compassion. We look to our parents for advice, for comfort and for peace. Most Christians are raised in the church because our parents instilled that inside of us, so that we can grow and always fall back on the word of God when we go astray. As we grow up and have a family of our own, the cycle continues. If parents are proud of how they've raised their children, then it would only be necessary to sit back and give them that same respect to raise the kids of their own. If you are going through a similar situation today, I say to you "lean not unto your own understanding but in all things acknowledge him and he shall direct your path." Our parents are dear to us and yes we must respect them. Know that clinging to your husband and wives does not mean that you don't respect your parents, or you are neglecting them. You can love them just the same. Making your own decisions and focusing on your family does not mean that you are a disobedient child. Any parent that would put their grown child in that position is not showing them unconditional love. In the bible it says love does not seek after oneself. Love is not selfish. Let go and Let God. You have to know that GOD is directing their path and he will not and can not fail. I've heard a friend tell me that her mother-In-Law was jealous of her and her husband's relationship and asked her son, "Well where I fit in your marriage?" If she reads Genesis 2:24 she would get a better understanding of the word and God's plan for our lives. Sometimes people don't understand things that happen on this earth but if they would just keep faith in the word and read, God will reveal his plan for our lives. Of course if you have parents who are not capable of taking care of themselves, it is only your duty to take care of them, like they did you all your life. If your husband and wife do not respect that, then they are not showing you unconditional love. God plants the word in our heart so that when situations like this occur, we will be able to move forward and glorify him in all that we do. I don't know what your situation is, or if you know someone who is having a difficult marriage because of their parents, but pray this prayer today for your strength in God as you search for peace in your family. God is able.

GENESIS 2:24

*"For this reason a man will leave his father and mother
and be united to his wife, and they will
become one flesh."*

Dear God,
Please hear the prayers
Of many couples today.
Those who want to become
One with their spouse,
But the parents are
Getting in the way.

Father we know
That we are to
Respect our parents
Forever,
But teach us how to
Separate ourselves
From their jurisdiction
So that our marriage
Will stay together.

Give our parents
The courage to let
Us go and live our
Own life.
Show them this is
Necessary for us
To become successful
Husbands and wives.

Father sometimes we
Feel as if we owe
Our parents so much
Today.
So it causes us to
Cling to them
And make us feel
Without them
We go astray.

Father show us
That your word
Commands us
To be faithful
To the
Marriage you

Bring together.
So that we can
Show our children
The meaning of
Love and how it
Will someday
Keep their families
Together.

For we know that
You will take care
Of our parents
When we are apart.
For them we will
Always have respect,
Compassion and
Thanksgiving in our
Heart.

Dear God,
By your word,
Through your word,
And in your word
We are truly blessed.
You said in your word,
"For this reason
 A man will leave his father and mother
And be united to his wife,
 And they will become one flesh"
AMEN

In My Father's House

I can recall when I was younger, my sister's uncle, Joe Dumars Sr. had passed away. He went to meet the Lord in Heaven. There was a famous family as many of you may know today, The Winans. They song a beautiful song at his funeral. It was called Millions Didn't Make it, but I was one of the ones who did. The song was talking about how many people don't make it in heaven, but at least I was one of the ones who did. It touched my spirit because we go through so much on this earth and we pray for our families as they travel this earthly road. Glory be to God to know and rejoice in the fact that there is a place far away from this world that we can have peace forever. The kind of peace that no man can take away. God has prepared a place for each of us who believe in his word. Our Salvation is won through faith. That is good news to know no matter what we do, God has rest for us that goes beyond any gift man can give in this life. Rejoice and be glad today. Do a good deed, Love someone, forgive someone today or simply just tell others about the goodness of God. One day we will meet him in heaven and we want him to be proud of us. Proud to say, here is your place that has been prepared. Go with gladness, knowing that you gave him your best in obeying his commandments. Pray this prayer for your strength in faith knowing that God has prepared a place for you in heaven and no one can take that away. God is able.

JOHN 14:2

"In my father's house are many mansions; if it were not so, I would have told you. I go to prepare a place for you."

Dear God,
    I know there is a place where pain is no more,
    Where my heart will rejoice like never before.

    A place that has my name written in stone;
    Where evil is unheard of and it's impossible to do wrong.

    A place where many angels call their home,
    So I can be at peace when I arrive and I'll never be left alone.

    It is a higher Kingdom that is prepared for the righteous soul;
    Not too high or too low, not too hot or too cold.

    A place that is just right- perfect in its creation.
    This earthly life is just a little stop to our final destination.

    Many get lost along the way and allow this world to hold them back,
    But Jesus I will not forget that you've prepared a place for me as long as I stay on the strait and narrow path.

    When and if you call my family and friends before me along the way,

Please help me to be strong and not question why you took their souls that day.

I know that I have sinned and fallen short of your glory,
But I'll keep looking for you because this earthly chapter is not the end of my story.

Dear God, I know the riches of this world will soon come to past.
In your kingdom you said, the last will be the first and the first will be the last.

So I know despite my struggles today, it will pay off in the end.
Once I'm in heaven I won't go through any tribulations again.

Thank you God for giving the world your son and everything he continues to do.
For he said, "In my Father's house are many mansions; I go to prepare a place for you."
AMEN

Oh Lord I Won't Complain

As a mother I now understood how my mom felt when we would always asked for things in the grocery store. My mom would get upset sometimes and say "NO". We would get angry and sad. Yet we didn't understand that she did so much for us throughout the week that it was never enough. Now having my own son, I see how she felt. I can buy him a toy every pay check. He would mistreat the ones I buy him and always want another whenever we go to the store. It seems as if you can never keep kids happy. When you don't give them things, they complain. No one wants to hear their children complain all the time. Surely you will get impatient and say "Go to your room, or be quiet!" Well I'm sure our God feels the same way. He can bless us so many times but we always find a reason to complain about the little things that life throws at us. Things that really doesn't matter. Things that may just be a test to see, if we are really ready for the bigger blessings he has in store for us. God wants to know that when the storm clouds come roaring down on us, we will be still and trust in him. When we complain and blame others for our problems we are separating ourselves from the fruit of the Holy Spirit, "faith love and happiness". Pray this prayer for your strength in the

Lord as you seek peace and restraint from complaining all the time. God is able.

PSALMS 106:24-25

"Yea, they despised the pleasant land,
they believed not his word:

25But murmured in their tents, and hearkened not unto the voice of the LORD"

Heavenly Father,
In the mist of my
Troubles how I want
To cry out and ask
You "why?"
It seems as if the
Devil is riding my
Back, making me
Angry as I cry!
It seems as if I
Can't catch a break
Throughout the day.
My money is low and
My friends don't have
Too much to say.
Just when I think there
Is light at the end
Of this dark road,
Another storm covers
My head and my warmth
Turns cold.

Dear God,
I just ask that
You give me the
Restraint I need
To wait on your
Blessings.
May I embrace
These troubles
Because I know there
Is no power in
Complaining nor
Stressing.
How easy it is,
To point the
Finger and give
Up on peace!
Father God I'm going
To ride this
Storm and allow
My faith to increase!
"This is broke,
I can't get this,
I can't do that!"
May all those phrases
Leave my mouth
So my light can
Come back!
Father I know
Others look at
Me and may not know
The troubles
I face.
Help me to
Still let the light
Of God shine in me,

So others will
Know my body
Is your dwelling
Place.
I will not
Murmer words
Of ungratefulness
Through this storm
And rain.
Give me the obedience
I need to keep still
And not complain!
AMEN

Old Time Religion

As I think about my grandmother it brings back many memories. I can smell the powder and the crème secret deodorant she used to use. I can smell the bacon and eggs cooking in the Kitchen while The Price is Right were on. Breakfast would be ready just in time for The Young and The Restless. Remembering on Sundays how she used to dress my sister and I for church. Our church was small. It was located on a dirt road full of rocks and mud. You would never know it was there if you were just driving by. The people would shout and dance. I never understood it. When I was little I thought these people had lost their mind. My grandmother also used to take us to funerals. She would dress my sister and I up alike. I can recall one funeral we went to, I asked my grandmother, "Ma why is she not moving?" She said, "Baby she's not here anymore she's gone to be with the Lord." I'm thinking to myself, "Okay, I know I'm just in the first grade and have a lot to learn, but I know that this lady is not gone anywhere, she's lying right in front of me!" Memories like those are simply priceless. Thank God for the grandparents who are still there for their grandkids today. Things are not the same. You don't find too many "Big mommas" today. When I think of strong grandparents, I think of a tree. Planted and rooted in deep soil. A grounded foundation to which many blessings and generations come from. That's why it is important for us to keep that "Old time Religion" tradition in our homes. If we plant God in our kids, they will grow and blossom to be the kind of Christians that God has called them to be. We all may stray away, as I know I have, but it will surely bring us back.   Read this poem for inspiration and pray for your strength in the Lord that you may be the kind of person to keep your family grounded in a Godly tradition. God is able.

ACTS 19:5

*"When they heard this, they were baptized in
the name of the Lord Jesus"*

Sweet Amazing Grace Melody from the early morn.
Testifying and praying of when sweet Jesus was born.

Feeling like the spirit is catching a hold of you.
Women in old hats crying as they pray
And dance the song through.

So much life in such a small wooden room.
The choir and the congregation humming an old
Spiritual tune.

The only instrument was that old organ sound.
Someone begin to faint,
So all gathered around.

Then we would go to the river,
All dressed in white.
As the preacher puts us in the water
We come up feeling new and bright.

Passing down that old country dirt road,
In pigtails and pink pantyhose,
Let the story be told.

There are many more churches being built today,
But things ain't what they used to be.
Just give me that old time religion,
It's good enough for me.
AMEN

Just To Be Close To You

I can recall when I was stationed in San Diego, California back in 2003. There was a chief at my job in whom I always would talk to because of his knowledge in the workplace as well as his spiritual wisdom. He once shared with me a statement his mentor would say to him all the time and that was, "Your experience will never out grow my wisdom." I found that statement very interesting as I was learning that many times people go through situations in their lives but some don't learn from their mistakes or they just don't get the lesson that is being conveyed. My mom told me that she has always prayed that GOD would put her children around people that would take care of us. I've personally always prayed that GOD would allow me to be an inspiration to others as he uses others to inspire me. Often times I found myself surrounded by people with wisdom and those with good sound hearts. It inspired me so to write and to gain strength. When you look at others and see the trials and tribulations that they have been through and yet they manage to grow from that and become successful, then it gives hope. It gives hope to the girl with no mother, it gives strength to the little boy with no father and it gives determination and faith to those of us who feel as if our obstacles are too hard to overcome. There was many times in which I wanted to hide things from my family and friends because I didn't want to bother them with my problems or because I felt as if I knew what was best in my own situation. When you carry a burden on your back for so long and doing so all by yourself, it grows heavy and it's a lot of stress to deal with. When I started opening up to others I learned that they had been down that same road, and the advice in which they had to share was all that I needed to move on. Many times when we have problems, GOD puts us around people who are knowledgeable about the things in which we are not so that they can help us. If we can just listen with our hearts instead of allowing the devil to whisper in our ear, "she or he can't help you because they are going through things themselves." I realized that I can't loose anything by just listening to someone talk. You'll know the wisdom of others through their heart. Knowledge is power and it is the American way. However, there is a difference between knowledge we learn in books and schools and wisdom. Wisdom is your key to living life; it is your key to relating to GOD and people. Have you ever noticed how older people just long for someone to sit down and talk to? When I visit my elders in Louisiana we sit outside on the porch all day just eating and talking. If you just listen to them it is their greatest joy. It's because they have lived life and they have a story to tell. They've been where the younger people are trying to get. Sometimes they laugh when we go on and on about our boyfriends and how we are going to plan out our lives. Surely they know that everything in life does not fall in place exactly as we think they would. "Just keep living baby." My grandmother would always say. I enjoyed talking to them because my heart and my mind would be refreshed when I would leave. I learned a lot as a young child just listening to my mother talk to her friends. She wouldn't hide much from us because she did not want us to go into the world blind and thinking life was a bundle of roses. When she would have bad experiences with her friends, she'd sit us down and talk to us. One thing I always remember she told me was this, "There are too many guys out there to date your friend's man and your man's friend. You have to set some type of standards about yourself." I always took that to heart and I remembered those words. I've had close friends betray me and would date guys that I used to or was still dating. I thought to myself, "Momma said there'd be days like this." Because my mom instilled so much in me as a young adult I could quickly point out things or people that were wrong in my life. My brain was like a sponge just ready to soak up all that I can get from the wise conversations of my elders. I know that life is very challenging and at times it can get the best of us, but to listen to others and know that there are solutions out there and ways to deal with the ups and downs of life just makes life somewhat sweeter. No matter how much you think you know, or how old you may be, you can never stop learning and gaining wisdom from others. Doctors, lawyers, judges and even parents, may not know everything there is to know about life so take time out of your busy day to share your wisdom with others and allow someone to be of good wisdom to you today. After all, talking for most of us is therapy for the heart. Wisdom shouts out from every angle of your life, but if you don't listen, you'll never hear her. The way in which our parents raise us, helps a great deal when it comes time to gain wisdom. We will know how to accept it and respect it. It's hard sometimes raising kids in this world. We get so busy and forget that those little brains need molding so that they can grow and gain wisdom from this mean world. Pray this prayer of Wisdom for your strength in the Lord. God is able.

PROVERBS 22:6

"Train up a child in the way he should go, and when he is old he will not depart from it."

Dear God,

Give me the wisdom I need to raise my child.

I know the lessons I teach him now will be his strength after a while.

For I too am human and will never have all the answers God.

But help me to instill in him patience and Faith when times get hard.

Help me to keep him in church as he grows,

Because when he needs it the most, your word he'll always know.

Please give me the direction I need to teach him your ways.

And show him how to never give up, even on those stressful days.

As it was written in the bible, may I live my life like a man who built his house upon a rock too,

That my son may see my foundation and so shall he also follow through.

May the mercy you have for me father, reflect the unconditional love I give my own

So that he may someday love his children even when they're wrong.

If you call me in your kingdom sooner than he can comprehend,

Allow your holy spirit to guide him to righteous people until we meet again.

Help me father to be strong when it comes time to let go,

So that he may find his own way in the world as he grows.

Sometimes it gets hard because for our children, we think we know what's best,

But you carried me through those dark nights and gave my heart a place to rest.

I know that the same things you did for me, for him you'll also do.

Fill him with your holy spirit so that his light may forever shine through.

But of all these things, I ask of you the most,

Give me the wisdom to train my child, to always keep you close.

AMEN

The Power Of Godly Leadership

As I have been in the military for 10 years, I know that Leadership is precious. It is like a gem. It is something that you cherish when you have hard times on your job. I can truly say that if you are not a child of God and you are not under good Leadership, you are like a small boat in a storm being tossed and driven. I know that sounds scary when you think about the physical aspect, but believe it or not, mentally it is worse. It's like your mind is that small boat drowning in the sorrows of this world. You can have the knowledge you need for your job, but if you don't have the common sense and the emotional care for your people, then all will fail. I came to learn that leadership is taking care of your people, it is getting out there working hard with your people; showing them that no problem they go through is too great for you to go through it with them. Leadership is letting your people know that you've been there and you sympathize with them. A Godly leadership is showing others how Jesus got down and washed the feet of man, just to show the world what they should do. How we should love and care for one another. Leadership is not a dictatorship but it's a privilege and all who are in that position should feel blessed to share their wisdom of God as well as their knowledge to uplift others. It's not about us, but it's about glorifying our Lord Jesus. If you are a leader, want to be a leader or just know a leader that you want to pray for, pray for your strength in the Lord as they move to the next level. God is able.

JOHN 13: 14-15

"If I then, your Lord and Master, have washed your feet; ye also ought to wash one another's feet. For I have given you an example that ye should do as I have done to you."

Dear God,
There are people fulfilling
Leadership positions
Across this nation.
Father cover them
With your wisdom
And patience.

Teach them how to
Be understanding
When it comes time
To hold others
Accountable.
Teach them not to
Discriminate and
May their words
Like you, be faithful.

Show them that when they
Take care of others,
People will follow.
Let their hearts
Be filled with compassion
And life instead of
Angry hollow.

May they humble themselves
And lead by example for all.
Looking to you for prayer,
And understanding their
Purpose and call.

For GOD we know
That if your son
Can wash the feet
Of men that sin,
Through Jesus
We too can.

Dear GOD,
Help someone to feel
The depth of your
Love as they pass
A helpless
Sister or brother.
You said in
Your word,
"If
I can wash your
Feet,
Surely you
Can do it for one another."
AMEN

Seeds Planted In The Soul

As a small child I remember how often my grandfather used to be on the road driving trucks. My grandmother always told me that he was in Texas. We used to sit outside of my grandparents snow white house and swing on that old wooden swing. Across the street from our house was this tall wooden fixture that looked like a large rectangular window. I used to look through that window and see cars passing by and to my imagination I thought that was Texas. I looked and anticipated my grandfather passing through that window on his way home. My grandfather was not home often. He was out working hard to provide for my grandmother and our family. He was a good man. One thing that I noticed about my grandfather was that he was a very quiet man. A man of few words. However, when words would grace his tongue, they would mean something special. My grandmother was very outspoken and most of the time we heard her around the house mad and voicing her opinion when he would upset her. It amazed me so because he used to just sit there and look at her rage on and on never once saying a word. My grandfather was a man of wisdom. If there was one thing he didn't like it was someone who had no common sense. I remember once I heard him say, "If you don't have anything nice to say, then don't say anything at all." Eventually my grandmother would calm down and see things clearly. My grandfather knew that adding fuel to her fire would only make things worse. Instead he continued to provide for the family and do things that kept his marriage to her, peaceful. When I think of my grandparents I can reflect on situations in my life when I were gentle and kind with my words and days in which I couldn't keep my mouth closed to save my life. When I was stationed on a ship back in 1999, there was a famous phrase that Sailors always used. Most of the time they were referring to me when they would use this phrase because they knew I couldn't keep a secret to save my life. It was "Loose lips sink ships." I used to work for the Captain of the ship so I knew everything that was going to happen before the crew knew. I was lucky enough to be around the Captain when he would talk and make decisions about our departures and arrivals. However, I knew that if I could relay this information to others, then I would gain the respect and attention of everyone on the ship. If I did this, I would be cool and admired by everyone. Well, when things were not going as planned and we would be out to sea longer than expected, I would tell the Sailors the bad news. I am the type of person that wants to know everything so I would listen and listen to other people's conversation. If I heard things that were bad, then I was happy to go and tell my friends. I was the gossip queen. It grew on me and I started doing it so often throughout my life. I thought it would make others happy that I could give them information that was hard to come by. As time went on and as I grew older, I realized by passing along all this bad information was making me just as guilty as the words I was repeating. When you are around negative situations and you keep that information flowing in your head and off your tongue, you stir those harsh and hatred ways up. I started feeling like people would think to themselves, "Here comes the gossip girl." It was fun and cool at first, but after a while I started putting myself in other people's shoes. Would I want people to spread bad things about me, especially if you didn't know for sure that it was true? GOD said, "So as a man thinks in his heart, so is he." Just keeping the information inside of me kept evil brewing in my heart. I did not like the person I had become. I started to change my life. I thought about my grandfather's words "If you don't have anything nice to say, don't say nothing at all." I was learning that if I stay quiet long enough to listen to what GOD is telling me, through others and Jesus, then I would be a messenger of good news. We have to be careful of even the news we listen to on Television as well. Too much negativity is not good for the soul. It starts growing in your spirit. Surround yourself around Godly things and Godly people so that everything around you will be of good news and blessings. Pray this prayer for your strength in the Lord for thinking good thoughts. God is able.

Proverbs 23:7

"For as a man thinks in his heart..............so is he."

A man plants in him many wicked ways unseen.
Yet with his slick tongue and riches around him
Appear so innocent and clean.

A man that plants bad seeds in his heart,
Curses his home and tears his family apart.

Dear God,
Help me to clear my thoughts of wicked thinking,
Because it is what comes out of my mouth that defiles
Me, not my eating or drinking.

I know that when I think negative thoughts,
It somehow travels deep within my soul.
Failure is what I'm creating and eventually

It will take its toll.

If my surroundings causes my thoughts to
Go astray,
Place my feet in holy places to re-new
My heart today.

Order my steps in your word God, so that I may seek wisdom through your son,
And that I may humble myself to be cautious of the words that grace my tongue.

Then shall I have the understanding when others plot evil thoughts against me,
With their slick smiles, thinking their wicked ways I won't see.
Your word clearly states "For as a man thinks in his heart…………..so is he."
AMEN

Serving God Alone

The bible tells us we are born with sin upon us and we have to be born again. In order to do so we have to let go of old ways and walk with Christ. There are things in our life that we enjoy so much and things in our lives that we don't want to get rid of even though we know it is holding us back in life. Especially at a young age, peer pressure causes many of us to stray away from GOD. Most of the time, the cool thing to do and places to go are full of temptation and evil. Growing up and trying to find your way in life you dip and dab in things that can convict your heart. The devil allows drugs and alcohol to do most of his work in this world. That is why the gate to destruction is so wide but "faith is the substance of all things hoped for and the evidence of things not seen". I'm learning today that if I keep my faith although this walk is narrow and hard to walk when many are not seeking eternal life, that I can make it. In the military constantly around others who are lonely. People don't understand the burdens of a Sailor; I've fallen with the rest of them. I've been in darkness when I couldn't see the light. In a world of a lost generation, I've been mis-used and I've mis-used others. I've walked through that wide gate many times, but Jesus always snatch me back and reassures me that my way and my walk is through the narrow passage. He directs my path when I can't find my own way. He is my truth and my light and If I can just keep myself discipline and steadfast, if I could just keep my faith towards the strait and narrow, I know that at the end my eternal life is waiting on me. I once heard a song that said, "I woke up this morning with my mind fixed on Jesus". Our God is a jealous God. We need to know that it's not about us, but it's about glorifying him and if something takes us away from that, it is not his will. Don't just say it, but pray this prayer for help to serve our God. God is good!

MATTHEW 6: 24

"No one can serve two masters; for either he will hate the one and love the other, or else he will be loyal to the one and despise the other. You cannot serve God and mammon"

Dear God,
Please help me to learn how
To discipline myself for your sake.
Help me to stay on the righteous path
And learn from my mistakes.
Dear Lord,
I am weak in the flesh and
Constantly go astray.
I'm trying to be loyal
To my bad habits,
Therefore I'm lacking
In praising you everyday.
It's impossible for
Me to be close to
You when I fall
For temptation.
Please help me

To be strong in
Your word so
I can give the
Holy Spirit my
Full dedication.
Oh Lord how I
Fool myself by
Thinking I can
Serve other things
As well as you,
Only to realize that
Your word is the
Only thing in my life
That can help me through.
Forgive me Father for
All those times I've
Served others and
Cared more about my pride.
Re-new my thoughts today
So I may reflect your
Light on the in and outside.
Father help us all
From getting caught up
In the fame and riches
Of this nation.
Some of us fall for money,
Some for other people.
Whatever may be the situation,
I pray for us all father,
Your children who are my sisters
And brothers.
Because you said,
"No one can serve two masters;
 For either he will hate the one and love the other."
AMEN

Suffering For Christ

If we pray and ask GOD to keep evil out of our homes and our workplace, he may move us or we may not stay at our job long but he has a way of removing us from that situation. Everything that looks bad isn't, and everything that shines is not gold. Many times we are so deep in sin that we don't have the strength and the spiritual guidance to see such evil prophets. The only way we can fight the devil is through the Holy Spirit and the only way we can receive what GOD has for us if we allow ourselves to be in position to receive the blessings and power he has for us. Many times I was out partying and having a good ole jolly time with the devil's workers that I couldn't stay sober long enough to know that the enemy was out to get me. All I knew was, I was cute and everyone wanted to get with me and be like me. I had a way of catching the attention of anyone I wanted and was not afraid to talk to people. The devil knew that I was a people's person, so he would bring people around who would try to stir me in the wrong direction. Women who were jealous of me and out to destroy me and get what I had. I was too confident and proud to see that they were plotting and planning against me. I was the life of the party, and I was a queen, no one could bring me down, so I thought. I soon found out that no matter who you think you are, GOD has a way of showing you that you are no better than anyone else. Jesus said, "If they prosecute me, then surely they will prosecute you." GOD had a way of showing me that it was time to come in from the fiesta. It's a time and a place for everything. There comes a time when you have to fall to your knees and humble yourself before the Lord, there comes a time when you have to walk by faith alone, there comes a time you have to call upon GOD, there comes a time when you have to put away your own selfish needs and ask GOD to order your steps in his word. Satan is busy and he continues to show up at our doorsteps like a wolf in sheep's clothing. If we are not constantly picking up the bible and receiving the word of GOD, we will go astray. Don't just say it, but pray this prayer for God to show you how to humble yourself to suffer for his name. Not as you will but as he will. God is able!

JOHN 15: 20

"Remember the word that I said to you, a slave is not greater than his master if they persecuted Me, they will also persecute you; if they kept My word, they will keep yours also."

When the world is against you and you can't go on another minute or hour,
Read the word of God to gain your strength and spiritual power.

For God said you would suffer for his name sake.
Keep your head up and have faith because our
Father in heaven, doesn't make mistakes.

You may grow hungry for his cause and be
Persecuted as well.
He will save you from the bondages
Of an earthly hell!
Yes, he will pick you up and carry you out
Because his word never fails.

Don't give up and ask
"Why Lord?" As you drown in sorrow.
Praise God during the stormy nights,
For he will comfort you and give you
Peace tomorrow.

When you are not of this world,
Struggles and troubles are promised,
So be patient and hold on.
Soon people will know you
Are a child of God and their
Evil ways can do you no harm.

For if you stumble and fall,
He will lift you high!
For if you are bruised and beaten,
He will be your medical supply!

Jesus is all and everything we need
In this world to survive.
Although we suffer for his name sake,
Through his promise,
Our spirit will never die.

"Oh ye of little faith,"
Always remember,
Hard times
We will go through.

Our heavenly father said,
"If they persecuted me,
I know they will persecute you."
AMEN

The Heavenly Journey

Matthew 5:4

*"Blessed are those who mourn,
for they will be comforted."*

"If anything happened to us, would you take care of Carmen?"
I still think of these words by my late cousin-in-law Deon
Jones. I remember him asking me that question in the car
as we passed The Power Center in Houston Texas. Deon
was killed a year later outside of a night club. He and my
cousin had divorced shortly before his death. He was like a
big brother to me. When I was living with my cousin in high
school I had grown close to Deon. His death not only affected
me but my entire family. Although he and my cousin agreed to
go their separate ways, he was still apart of our family, at least
in my heart he was. Carmen is my little cousin, his daughter.
She was truly his gem. He treasured her more than anything
in this world. Because of his death I've always felt like I was
forever in his debt to ensure that Carmen's life remains on
track. Life sometimes throws these curve balls at us out of no

where. You never see the tragedy coming. I never thought he would die because he was so full of life. Everyone loved to be around him. Deon could step into a room and own it. His presence was known from the moment he stepped into a crowd. When you wake up one day and someone so special like that is taken away from you, it hurts. It hurts deeply. Before these things happen to us we always feel as if we couldn't go through it. I'm here to say that Jesus knows how much we can bear. When we lose people that are special to us, he is right there to pick us up. I felt weak and he renewed my strength. He knew what it took to get my strength right again and Jesus did just that. When you feel like you can't go on anymore, he will touch you. He will pick you up and carry you over that mountain. Nothing is too great for him to handle. People come into this world for a reason. When God's will is fulfilled throughout our lives, we must journey to heaven when we're called. Our selfish ways tells us that we need them on earth today. However, Jesus has plans for us individually. Life is a gift and we should treat it as such. Just because someone is no longer with us physically, does not mean that this world will not continue to go around. There are lessons to be learned from every tragedy. Like he said, "there is a blessing in the storm". We have to figure out what it is. I thought about what he would want me to do with my life if he could speak to me. I know he would want the best for me. When I feel like giving up, I think of Deon. He would say, "Don't quit." Jesus wants us to mourn and always remember those who have made an impression in our life because there are blessings to be given from our tears. Always keep those memories alive in your heart and spirit. Although that physical presence may be gone we can keep dreams and others love alive in our hearts. Many times when we lose people that are dear to us, it actually motivates us to do more in life. It will make you reach high as the stars. Do not let the troubles of the world stir you on the wrong path. Jesus said "Weeping may endure for a night but joy comes in the morning light." When you are down and think about the death of your love one, know that you are here for a purpose. Know that GOD has kept you around today for a reason. Do something special with your time on this earth. Tomorrow is not promised. If you die tomorrow will you be satisfied with the things you have accomplished your time on this earth? As I think of Deon and the time I shared with him. I'm remembering how he made others laugh. I once heard someone say, "Laugh often, it adds joy to the heart." I think of how he opened his home to me. Jesus said, "Do unto others as you would have them do unto you." I also think of how he loved with his whole heart. Jesus said, "Love others as I have loved you. By this, they will know that you are my children." Yet he may have had goals and dreams he never got to accomplish, I truly believe he did what God sent him to do. I'll forever keep him in my heart as his memory gives me strength. Always look towards the hills for your strength. Jesus said "Let not your hearts be troubled." Appreciate the times you spend with family and friends. Take time out to call them and say I love you. Take pictures often to cherish memories. Talk more after work and before going to bed. It may be something you say to them that keeps them smiling or keeps their heart beating for one more day. Death is something we can't escape. Yet with Jesus help we can deal with the loss of our loved ones. As it is written, "Blessed are those who mourn, for they will be comforted." Pray this prayer for your strength in the Lord when others cross to the holy land. God is able.

1 Thessalonians 4:17

"Then we which are alive and remain shall be caught up together with them in the clouds, to meet the Lord in the air: and so shall we ever be with the Lord"

Dear God,
Please comfort those who
Are afraid to loose their love ones today.
Heavenly father put your armor of protection
Around the family and wipe their tears away.

Dear Lord,
Let them know that a physical
Death is only the beginning of forever.
Lord you said that the spirit will
Never die, but only bring heaven
And our loved ones together.

When we die, we meet you
Lord and your heavenly son Jesus Christ.
We will have no sorrow, no pain and
No disturbing memories of this life.

Father, we all fail to remember
That you said this life is a gift from you.
Our days here are numbered and
We will have eternal peace when
This earthly journey is through.

So often do we get caught up in
Worldly things and our selfish
Ways,
But father you said seek your
Kingdom first and give you all
the praise.

Jesus hold your children
and give them peace in
their hearts while they grieve.
Even those who are

about to passover,
give them the strength to
leave.

Yes, we must remember
we are all your children
and you have prepared
many mansions for
us all.
When you are ready to
give us eternal happiness,
we must answer to your call.

Oh sisters and brothers,
dry your eyes, thank God and be
proud!
Jesus said,
"Then we which are alive and remain
shall be caught up together with them in the clouds."
AMEN

The Lord's House

Many times in our life we have to travel from time to time. In our travels we fail to find a church home that we can lay our burdens down. So busy, just not enough time to even go to church. Until that one day, that day that God just strips you of everything. You have nothing, no one to turn to, no where to go. So you reflect on your childhood and how the Church played a major role in your grandparents strength. Not understanding it so much when we were younger, yet as we grow older we realize that we need the church. Not the physical presence as much as the mental nurture. You can let go of the past at the church, at the altar. God has a word for you in the church. God has a plan for your future in the church. Praying anywhere is sure to keep you close to the Lord, but he will direct your path and make your vision clearer if you place yourself in the church. Being obedient means placing yourself in the right position to receive your blessings. The church is this place. Maybe you are searching for a church home right now. Pray and ask God to find a church that will bring out the best in you. When Solomon built the first church he prayed that this would be the place that all of God's children can find rest and relief. Thank God for our churches today. Pray this prayer for your strength in the Lord as you search for or simply appreciate your church home. God is able.

1 KINGS 8:28

"Yet regard the prayer of Your servant and his supplication, O LORD my God, and listen to the cry and the prayer which Your servant is praying before You today: 29 that Your eyes may be open toward this temple night and day, toward the place of which You said, 'My name shall be there,' that You may hear the prayer which Your servant makes toward this place. And may you hear the supplication of your servant and of your people Israel, when they pray toward this place. Hear in heaven your dwelling place; and when you hear, forgive."

A place where I can lay my burdens down with ease.
A place where I seek comfort and peace.

A home away from home in my time of need,
Whether I'm traveling state to state or overseas.

Dear God when we enter your house the
Holy Spirit has a way of bonding people together.
When King Solomon built the first
Temple you said you would dwell there forever.

Dear God this world can really make us
Feel cruel and alone,
But when we go to the altar to pray
You give us strength to move on.

When I enter this holy place I feel
Your presence so deep.
We sing and praise,
We laugh and we weep.

When I fall short of sin and
Stray away from the church family,
It's good to know that no matter
How bad it gets, the doors of
The churches are always open to me.

Although many false prophets are
Seen lurking in this holy place,
Just grant us the wisdom to
See their evil face.

For many are discouraged today also
Because tithes and offerings have
Become a great debate,
But teach us to realize this
Fellowship does
Not have a 10% fixed rate.

For you said Give to the poor and
Give from your heart too.
But Let us remember that
Loving one another is
The best gift we can give you.

May you be with us until we meet again,
In your house Lord, where I bury my sins.
AMEN

The Race of Life

I remember the winter of 2003 when I was stationed in San Diego California. I gave birth to my son that summer and had gained 70 pounds that I was determined to loose. The odds were against me medically. I was having problems with my leg from the delivery. I was told it could take up to a year before I regained the strength in my leg. I was very disappointed because I had a newborn that I wanted to be able to get around for and protect. I felt as if the weight on my leg made it worse. I had a plan. I stuck to it faithfully. I couldn't run for the first couple of months. I went to the gym early every morning and exercised for 45 minutes. The Navy requires us to work out 3 times a week but I did it 5 and sometimes seven. I was on a strict diet. I learned to disciplined myself. Eventually I started regaining strength in my leg and I know it was because I was working out. As soon as it grew strong enough, I ran every day at lunch. I was seeing great progress. I was proud of myself. It was times when I was the only one running on certain days but it didn't bother me because I knew I had a goal for myself and my body. It reminded me of a motivational poster that used to hang in my office and it read, "There's never a crowd on the extra mile." The poster was a picture of a man running all by himself. When I think about determination, discipline and personal devotion, I think about walking with Jesus to eternal life. For he said narrow is the way to life and only few will find it. Doing the right thing may seem easy to some people at certain times but in a world of so much evil and temptation it is so easy to stray away from God's will. Simple things such as food. My favorite foods are the unhealthiest for my body. That's life. The things which are good to us are really wrong for us. You have to really discipline yourself and stay focus on your goals in life because each day is a battle. For GOD said wide is the gate and broad is the way that leadeth to destruction and many will find it. Keep your eye on the prize and look ever towards heaven because God's word is everlasting. Even when it seems like you can't make it, know that God is able. Don't just say it, but pray this prayer for strength to keep on keeping on. God is good.

PROVERBS 3: 5-6

"Trust in the lord with all your heart
And lean not on your own understanding;
In all your ways acknowledge him
And he will make your path straight."

Dear God,

In this walk of life teach me to not put all my trust in man.

Show myself and others the importance of leaving all our burdens in your hand.

For at times we fall out the race and expect others to help us back on our feet.

However, many times they are too busy traveling their own path in life and in our different travels we will never meet.

But I know you have set the path for each of us before we came

Into this life.

Sometimes we think we know what's best for us and really in our minds we think its right.

Yet it takes time, experience and wisdom just for some of us to give good advice.

But only you know what's best for us and can guide us through your son Jesus Christ.

Father I look to you for my strength to pick me up and put me back in this race.

I will praise and glorify you always not worrying about my neighbor and if he is in first place.

For each of us have our own way, yet we all shall seek your righteousness first.

You said if we do so you will give us strength when we're tired and water when we thirst.

I won't stop running even when I can't see the end.

I won't give up when I fall short of sin.

I won't allow my past and my fears to hold me back.

I won't allow my own understanding to continuously knock me off track.

Father you said that the race is not giving to the swift, but the one who endureth to the end.

I know if I just keep my faith and eyes on you, I will win.

We are weak in the flesh and sometimes it causes our hearts shame,

But I know with you I can make it to the finish line, and there in the book of life shall be my name. There should be my name.

AMEN.

The Silent Prayer

I had a dream that I was in the bathroom preaching to a group of people. I can recall so clearly in my dream a lady asked, "What does it mean to be intimate with God." I told her being intimate with God is spending time with him praying. Many people shy away from prayer because they are afraid that the way in which they pray is not good enough for the Lord. I told her how well God knows our hearts. We do not have to use big and fancy words to get our point across. Speak from your heart and ask with faith. Know that what you ask God for he will deliver. Then the question came up as to when and where to pray because they had such a busy schedule. I remember saying, "I spend time praying in the bathroom during the day. When you go to the restroom most of the time you are alone and you can just call on the name of Jesus and worship him in your heart. The most important thing you can do is spend time alone with God. Some people go to the beach, some go driving, some go to the park, and some just go in a room." I once heard an old spiritual song and it went as followed, "Come on in this room. Jesus is my doctor and he writes out all my prescription, he gives me all my medicine in a room." God is everywhere you invite him. Spend time alone with him and get to know him. You'll know that he is the great I am.

You don't have to stand at the alter, or preach to thousands, or read the dictionary to communicate with him. God knows each of us and calls us by name. Pray for those who do good things to be recognized by men because God knows when no one else does. Pray this prayer for your strength in the Lord as you serve him whole-heartedly and in private. God is able.

MATTHEW 6:6

"But when you pray, go away by yourself, shut the door behind you, and pray to your Father in private. Then your Father, who sees everything, will reward you"

Dear God,
 Please help me to understand
The importance of praying.
Sometimes we panic when we
Go through trials instead
Of listening to what you are
Saying.

In your word you teach us to
"Ask and you shall receive".
Heavenly father that goes
Out the window for most
When we are convicted and
When we grieve.

It takes time and prayer
To have faith in you
God.
Although when you
Gave your life for us
On the cross,
To you-that wasn't
Hard.

How dare we
Expect so much
Forgiveness as
We sin.
We thank you
God for having
Mercy on us,
Inspite of
This evil
Flesh deep
Within.

Yet, through prayer,
We can glorify you
And claim your faith
As we live.
By prayer we
Are blessed with
Peace and by
The testimonies
That others give.

By prayer we
Can save the people
We love from
Going to hell.
By faith, we can
Uplift the poor
And those
Struggling
In Jail.

Father, let
Us not be so
Anxious to
Gloat
To our sisters
And brothers,
But in silent
Prayer, give glory
To each other.

For we know pride
And arrogance is
Not your will.
God help us to
Be humble and
In your name,
Keep still.

For those who tell
The world what they
Have done,
Will only receive
Thanks
Through an earthly
One.

But GOD
Because of my
patience you reward
me and never give
up on my soul.
When we pray,
Pray in private,
And our rewards
Will be ten fold.

Father your word
Is so faithful
And true,
You said in your word,
be
Private in prayer,
"Then your Father,
Who sees everything, will reward you"
AMEN

The Toolbox To Jesus

Have you ever opened an appliance box that was full of tiny pieces? You look at the picture on the outside of the box and try to figure out how to put it together. If you are like me I don't like to read instructions well. Most of the time I try to just look at the picture and put it together but I always fail. Somehow I fail to realize that there are small details that you can't see on the picture that is listed in the instruction book. Well it reminds me of Jesus and the route in which we need to take to get to him. Many times we try to go around life's shortcuts because we are impatient or simply because we feel we are too busy and don't have time to pray and go to church. We may find comfort for the moment and we may make it through for a little while, but sooner or later we will be like a vehicle that has ran out of gas. Jesus said he is "the way and the truth and the life". Meaning there is no other way, there is no getting around Jesus unless you are lying to yourself because he is the truth and only can you find eternal life through him. Many times we know we need to follow Jesus but we try to put it off for so long because we are not ready for what comes along with taking that big step. Walking with Jesus means being true to yourself first because if no one else sees or knows all, he does. We can lie to others and we can paint a perfect picture for the world to see, but nothing gets passed him. He knows our thoughts before we think them. I know many times it is hard for me to ask for forgiveness for the things in which I was afraid I would do again. Jesus said "go and sin no more." That "no more" part just gets to us sometimes. You can't play with GOD and you have to really mean what you say to him because he knows your heart and he knows if you are faithful in your walk with him. When I come before GOD and ask for forgiveness I also ask him to take away that urge and that temptation that causes me to sin. There is power through prayer and through prayer you can overcome any of life's obstacles. When you reach a certain age in your life you realize that you can't keep going around Jesus because he is the only way out. Yes, at times it will be dark and cold but he is the light. He will show you the way and let his light guide you to eternal happiness. "No one comes through the father except through me." Jesus is our ticket to heaven. WE must work for our place through the Holy Spirit. All that he asks is that we believe and tell others of his glory. There were times when I was broken and bruised from the heartaches and terror of life's wicked rage but at the minute and hour when I was weak, Jesus touched me and he showed me that my joy was not of this earth and that my final journey was not of this world but heaven. I stand on his word and it is my shelter in the storm. Each day I hunger for wisdom and guidance from Jesus because I know that it will lead me to the father.

PROVERBS I: 28

"They will come to me but I will not answer.
They will look for me, but will not find me."

Dear Heavenly father,

I come to you today in truth and honesty as I confess my sins.

I have allowed the temptation in the world today to break me in.

I disobeyed your word and at the same time, knew in my heart it was wrong.

Because I am human and of the flesh, I became weak instead of remaining strong.

I allowed the hate and actions of others to make me judge and talk about my enemies who despise me.

Therefore causing you to cut off my blessings instantly.

For clearly your word states, be obedient and steadfast and I will make your enemies your footstool.

Instead I used my tongue and evil thoughts to react and think like a fool.

Although people may plot against me and try to make my patience short.

I should always seek your guidance and understanding when I feel like things are falling apart.

Father I now realize that when I do evil of any kind,
I allow negative energy to conquer this path of mine.

Even if it never seems to be my fault, there is a reason why I'm close to sin.

You always show me what I'm doing wrong and get me back on track again.

We are from the earth and so our understanding is earthly,

But you are high as the heavens and so is your understanding heavenly.

Therefore, I know I can't make it in this life without your word and your love.

I ask that you plant my feet back on solid ground so that I can gain wisdom from above.

Teach me to be steadfast and hold on to your word even at the darkest hour,

For it is then that you will call upon blessings to overflow like a running shower.

Yes, it is me father, standing in the need of prayer today.

Forgive me for my sins and with your son Jesus let them be washed away.

Lord restore my soul and mind with new thoughts, so that my heart can clearly see.

For you said in your word that sinners, "They will call to me, but I will not answer. They will look for me, but will not find me."

AMEN.

The Will of God

Have you ever been in a relationship and you knew it was not right for you, but you didn't want to let it go. You wanted to make him/her for you? Well I have as well. I once heard an old spiritual song and the lyrics were as followed, "Lord don't move this mountain, but give me strength to climb it, Lord don't remove this obstacles, but give me strength to overcome them." That really touched my spirit because so often we want God to do specific things for us. We want to be with this person and we want God to agree with us. We want this job and we want God to say it is the right one. We want this house even if we can't afford it, but we want God to make a way. Bless our little hearts. We have to know that we are of this earth so our way of thinking is earthly, God is higher than the heavens and so his way of thinking is. We may not understand why our situations exist but we must have faith in God and know that everything works together for the good of God and those who are called according to his purpose. Even when people get ill and we just can't understand because they are such good people. Maybe you prayed for them and used the phrase, "By his stripes you are healed." Yet that person is still sick. My pastor once said, things happen to people for a reason, he will give them strength to make it through. God may have allowed sickness and disease in the lives of people, but he clearly states, "My mercy and grace is sufficient." He will have mercy on all of us if we just follow him even when it is hard. We have to let go of the way we want our lives to be and start living for God. Jesus said it best when he gave his life so that he may have mercy on us, "Not as I will but as you will." As you read this inspirational poem. Pray for your strength in the Lord in doing his will and not yours. Be aware of conviction from the Lord. God is able.

I asked the Lord to send me someone
I can call my own.
He sent me courage and faith to be strong.

I asked the Lord to send me someone I
Could relate to.
He sent me a reflection of myself
Through you.

I asked the Lord to keep us happy and
Married forever.
He sent challenges for us to face
Together.

I asked the Lord to give me a sign
When it was time to let you go.
He gave me several signs but my heart
Kept telling me "No".

And now you've hurt me once again, and
I asked the Lord, "Why?"
He responded, "Because my will is not your own
My child."

Victory Today Is Mine

As a young child I remember wanting to go to the amusement park Kings Dominion when we lived in FT Meade Maryland. I remember my sister saying, "We're going to King's Dominion!" At the time I wanted to believe her, but it was just too good to be true. I had to have confirmation. I had to hear it from the person who would actually be taking me, my mom. I ran downstairs and my mom said, "Go get dressed, we are going to King's Dominion." To hear those words from her was my ticket to happiness. I knew that it was the truth. As I think about God's grace and his promise to the world, I think about a joy that this world can't even speak of. The promise that was written in the bible is the confirmation to the world that no matter what we say and do in this life, if we just believe GOD sent his son to pay the ultimate price for our sins. John 3:16 said it best For GOD so loved the world, that he gave his only Son, that whoever believes in him should not perish but have eternal life" That confirmation is our ticket to heaven! Just to think that he loved the world so much that he would give his son as an exchange for our sins should be reason enough to walk in an upright path in life! No matter what you are going through today, you need to rejoice and be glad. Victory is yours through Christ Jesus! The price is already paid and it is written. Don't just say it, but pray this prayer through the storms and the trials. God is good!

I Corinthians 15:57

"But thanks be to God, who gives us the victory through our Lord Jesus Christ."

The devil is a liar,
And he is put to shame before
Men.
He tried and tried,
But I would not allow him
To come into this heart of mine.

He's been camping out and he s been
Plotting all day long.
But thanks be to God, that I have
The tools I need to depend on God's word
And stand strong.

He knew my weakness and tried to
Use it against me as I did God's will.
Little did he know that I had the faith
Of David and the Holy Spirit he can
Never Kill!

When I woke up this morning
With Jesus on my mine,
I had the strength and determination
To kick the devil's behind!

I walk with my head held high,
And Satan can't stand my pride,
He tried to sneak into my house,

But I cast him out and with my
Grace made him step aside!

I've got plans to do things
Today and Jesus is driving me
So honey I'll be just fine,
Cause I told Satan that
Victory today is mine!

I'll move any, who will get in my way,
And because of his promise, this
Mission I won't think twice,
The bible says,
"But thanks be to God, who gives us the victory
 Through our Lord Jesus Christ"
AMEN

Welcome Lord

Have you ever gone to someone's house and they didn't make you feel welcome? I can recall a time when I went to one of my friend's house and her parents were having a bad argument. They weren't yelling but you could feel the tension as you walked in. My friend was telling me that it was okay to come and sit down. They were about to have dinner. The parents did not ask me if I wanted anything. I was so hungry because we had a long day. I felt very uncomfortable. My friend's mom started yelling at her because she was mad at her husband. I left because I didn't want to be in such hostile environment. Sometimes we get so upset at things that are happening in our life that we stray away from God. God said "Let your light shine so bright before men that they may see your good works and acknowledge the father in heaven." When you have guest in your home you want them to feel welcome. No matter what you may go through welcome others because God shines in you when you care for others. This pleases him. Our body is like a home for Jesus. Our spirit. God was talking to me the other night in a dream. I was getting into a confrontation with a young lady who was stationed on the ship with me as I was serving in the US Navy. In my dreams the girl pushed me. I had a chance to walk away, but I felt like everyone would think I was afraid. Before I laid a hand on her, I knew that we both would be in trouble if I were to fight her. Knowingly, I did anyway. I felt it more important what people would think. Sometimes we have to forget what the world thinks about us because when we walk with Jesus we will be different. God answers those who are obedient in his word. If we look for rewards from this earthly world, that would be our reward, but when we seek comfort in Jesus his mercy and grace endureth forever. Invite him in your home today as you love and care for others. Invite him in your soul and in your spirit today so that he will have comfort in knowing that you will carry out his will. Pray this prayer for strength in the Lord as you seek God even in the midst of your trials. God is able.

LUKE 11:9

"And I say unto you, Ask, and it shall be given you;
seek, and ye shall find; knock, and it
shall be opened unto you."

Dear God,
I'm sending you an invitation today.
Not because I'm broken or because
I have bills I need to pay.
I'm asking you to come and
Fill this room with your holy
Spirit and voice.
I welcome you today,
To show you thanksgiving
And because I decided
To make your will a priority
And not a choice.
Come today Lord and
See how I humble
Myself in your

Presence and
Shout and sing!
Today I honor you
And give you
Thanks for all
Things.
You are King of
My life and I
Know you are
Working miracles
Our right now! I don't know
What you will do
But I know
you will come through
some way, some how.
I put my faith in you
God because you
told me to stand still.
The unbelievers you
will save and the
sick you will heal!
There's no limit to your
power, so we
 show no limit to
your honor as tears
fall down my thankful face.
So I welcome you
in this place.
Come, come Lord and
renew my spirit through and
through!
For you said in your
word,
"Knock and the door
shall be open unto you."
AMEN

When A Man Finds A Wife

I truly believe that the most difficult thing in life is choosing a mate. So many times when we date and meet people in the beginning of the relationship they are the perfect person. Especially if you are in a relationship, or just getting out of a bad relationship; it seems as if the person you are dating is everything that the other person wasn't. As I lived and learned I realized that when we are in our early stages of dating and falling in love, we spend most of our time trying to seem like angels and impressing our mate until we paint a picture that we just can't live with for the rest of our lives. No matter who you are, you have flaws. Some are different than others, but flaws will be there. How do we choose a mate? How do we pick someone that we want to spend the rest of our lives with? How do we pick someone that would want to spend the rest of their lives with us? I learned in my first marriage that love was not enough alone to marry someone. I can recall when my ex-husband first asked me if I was sure that I wanted to get married. My response was, "I know because I love you. I know I do!" Little did my naive heart and mind know that there was so much more to being married. Love is good and you must love someone to spend the rest of your life with them, but if you don't have patience and a forgiving heart, then you have nothing. When we marry someone we are agreeing to go through life with that person in a partnership. No matter what happens to either one of you or what you do, you are willing to stay together. That "for better or worse" is a vow that most of us don't take seriously. Someone has to be grounded and need to have GOD in their life. The link to keeping two people bonded together is Jesus. He will work through you to heal and keep your relationship. We must put GOD first and he'll do the rest. Relationships are just like anything else in life, if it's not God's will it will not last long. You can be the prettiest, most handsome, smartest, richest, or whatever that person desires, if GOD doesn't feel that you make a perfect match, you will not be together long. I learned to pray and ask GOD to help me work out my relationship only if it is his will and to order our steps if this is his will for us to be together. I know that my patience was short and I was ready to walk away when I felt like I was not getting the attention I deserved. When you are in a marriage you stand by your man/woman no matter what they do to you. You forgive them because you know that they may be going through life's trials and tribulations. The bible says that love is "unselfish" meaning you put your lover before yourself. Not too many people who marry in this generation, is willing to put someone else before them. Especially when we are young. When we are young we think we have life figured out but the truth is, we are still learning a lot. If we are in a relationship at this time, then we force our lover to go through the learning phase along with us. However, that is a big part of love and marriage. This world we live in teaches us that cheating on our husband/wife is unheard of and if it happens you should divorce him/her. A marriage should not fall apart because of infidelity. You should forgive your mate and try to find out what went wrong. You should get counseling for your marriage and try to heal the wounds. It's easier said than done, but if it's God's will, you will survive together. No one said that the road would be easy.

Many times when we are having relationship problems it could be from something that we are not doing or something we are doing that causes our mate to do wrong. Communication is a key factor in relationships. If you can't open up to your husband or wife, then it makes it difficult to work problems through. Not saying that cheating is ever a way out or a solution, but we are human and it does happen. I also learned that there is no problem too great to work through with your mate as long as they are giving you the same energy as you are giving them. A famous singer Teddy Pendergrass once said it best, "sometime I've given 40 and she's given 60, or sometimes I've given 70 and she's given 30, but you just don't know how good it feels to have someone who loves you the same, talking about a 50/50 love." If you have a man that is there no matter what you do, no matter what your faults are he will always look at you like his queen, then you stay with that man forever. If you find a woman that stands behind you and treats you like the king that you know you are or could be, then you keep her because she is your treasure. Many times we may grow tired of the same arguments and the same person all day everyday and when we go out in the world the devil temps us. You look at those beautiful and handsome people at the store and at the bar. They seem to be everything that your husband or wife isn't and you grow curious. I know because I've been there. You must know that those same people are getting on someone else' nerves too. Its human nature for us to be curious and wonder "what if" but there comes a time when we need to appreciate what GOD has given us. Many times when I was out, whether it is at a grocery store, work or at a party; I've had guys approach me and say, "Your man is a lucky man". It upsets me a little because they have no idea what my man goes through for me. He works hard for my love. He earned my love. I am only human and I have my faults. I drive him crazy at times. The reason I am with him, is because no matter what I do and say he stands by my side. I know that no matter what, he will be there for me. It takes a strong man to stand by a strong woman and he does it so well. As much as men try and say things and do things to prove to me that they would love to be in my man's shoes, I know in my heart that no one could possibly love me as much as my man. When a man loves and respects his woman through thick and thin, he is a good man. When a woman does the same, they are meant for each other. For we know we all have faults and will experience failure some point in our life, but to have patience and forgiveness towards each other will keep your relationship afloat. Trust your mate before you doubt him/her, admire one another, and keep the fire burning and the lines of communications open. One of my closest childhood friends married a girl that he loves and cherish to this day. He gave her the world. However, he fell on hard times one year and she wasn't strong enough to stand by his side. She blamed him for her financial situation and anything negative that she could through in there. She went straight into the arms of another man. A man in whom she thought would give her all that she dreamed of. How quick she realized that this man had faults just like anybody else, yet she would rather deal with her husband's old problems than another man's new problems. Luckily he allowed her back into his life. My question to him will always be, "Can you honestly say, if you fall on hard times again for a moment, will your wife leave you again?" Hard times will come in a marriage and it is those very times that will test your relationship. Anyone can stick around for the sunshine, but to be there when the storm clouds are roaring, you know that you have something so special in that person that is hard to come by. Many people have gone through life just fine without having a husband or wife by their side. However, to have a partner to help you tackle life's problems makes life a little easier. Men, embrace your woman and make her feel beautiful because we love to feel sexy and like we are queens. Women, don't deceit and betray your man as soon as problems occur. Men need to know that we will be strong and we will stand by them even through the toughest times. When we are married and give ourselves to other men, no matter the situation, he feels like he has nothing left. You were his pride possession. Something he could be proud of and you take that away when you make bad decisions. Always take care of home. Make home a place where he wants to come. His safe place away from the worries of the world. A place where he can rest and feel at ease. If the home is a hostile place, he may find comfort in other homes. I have made some childish decisions in my life, but I think GOD I've learned how to be a good woman in the end. He'll know when the time is right; he'll know by the way she carries herself. Jesus said it best, "When a man finds a wife, he finds a good thing."

PROVERBS 18:22

"He who finds a wife, finds a good thing"

A man that finds a wife has found someone who he can pray with at night.
A man that finds a wife, has found someone who will inspire him to do what's right.

A man, who finds a wife, has found a friend, lover and a soul-mate.
A place of warmth he can run to in a world full of frustration and hate.

Someone who may know his fault, yet accept him with all that he is inside and out.
When he makes mistakes, she'll be that calm and peaceful strength instead of a noisy shout.

When a man finds a wife, he has found a woman who finds strength also in the word.

A woman that will stand by his side despite the negative opinions she may have heard.

When a man finds a wife, he has found someone who will pick him up when he falls.

Someone who will stand by his side with grace ever so strong and tall.

Yes, when a man finds a wife, he has found a jewel, a diamond and a pearl.

When he looks at her he sees love and she is the center of his world.

For when a man finds a wife, he finds peace within his soul,

Someone he can talk to for hours and in hopes they can grow old.

But most of all, when a man finds a wife, he is closer to the heavenly father above,

Because when a man finds a wife, together they shall reflect the power of God's love.

A man, who finds a wife, finds a new love song
To loudly sing,
For the bible tells us,
"He, who finds a wife, finds a good thing."
AMEN

When The World Forgets Me

He'll lead you out the pit of jealousy, the pit of financial burdens, the pit of low self-esteem and the pit of drug abuse. Jesus knows your heart. He knows your fears. Whatever it takes to bring you out, he will do. He may not do it in a way which is pleasing to you, but a way in which will change your life forever. I realized many times that Jesus talks to us at different times, and in different voices. What may work for my friend, may not work for me and when he talks to my friend, he may not be talking to me. Because my grandmother instilled that foundation of Faith in my heart, I know his voice. I know when he's talking to me and I know when he is calling my name. We must answer him when he calls. Sometimes we have to take ourselves away from the things in which we used to do and the people in which we used to surround ourselves with. I'm not saying my friends were bad, but GOD was speaking to me as an individual and I knew it was time to isolate myself in order to receive the blessings he had for me and in order to do his will. We all have gifts from GOD. Many of us may not know, or may not wish to discover that which GOD has placed before us to teach and reach out to other people. He has his way of allowing us to make that choice in life. I just refuse to ignore him because he has been so good to me. When I was left with nothing inside my heart, in my soul, when my way of thinking was small, he renewed my thoughts and he has taken me from a place in which I was headed to hell. I've found that when you walk close with Jesus then the temptation of the world just eats away at you. The devil knows what tempts you and he will use that to his advantage because he knows our weakness. I know that if I just keep my head lifted towards Jesus, if I just keep walking down that narrow path, if I just keep doing things which are pleasing to the Lord like treating others with love and respect and if I keep reading the word, I will have the power I need to defeat the devil. Thou I walk through this valley, I will stand still like a rock and let my faith guide me through. I know the people around me can't carry me; I have to walk this walk on my own. I thank GOD that he gives me strength the more I pray. If you have Jesus in your life you don't have to lean towards drugs or people because his word is strong enough to stand on alone. Don't just say it; pray this prayer for spiritual power. God is good!

GALATIANS 6:9

"Let us not become weary in doing good, for at the proper time we will reap a harvest if we do not give up."

Dear God,
Please help me to continue shining my light,
Every where I go.
When I enter a place of business, let the
Goodness of my heart always shows.

At times when everyone is against me,
And laughing at the things I do.
Help me to keep a clear head and
Continue to glorify you.

In the workplace, where I reside
Most of my days,
Give me the strength to
Work hard consistently,
Even when the devil tries to
Get in my way.

When I'm looking for
Rewards and justice for
The deeds that I accomplish in
Faith,
And no one seems to notice
Or even step in to give me a
Break,

Help me to not look for
The world to reward me all the time,
You said that your reward is much
Greater than our human lives can
Ever find.

Help me to look ever forward,
And praise you in faith and
Through your word.

For, I've seen your miracles
In work,
And your voice of comfort,
I've heard.

Although sometimes my
Heart tells me
How others do me wrong and "if
Only he or she would…….."

Through my sweat,
Pain and tears,
I will not grow weary
In doing good.
AMEN

Why Do We Hate So Good?

JOHN 8:7

"If any one of you is without sin, let him be the first to throw a stone at her."

As I write my thoughts today, I am reminded of my daily struggles within myself trying to walk a straight and narrow path. A couple of days ago I was having an argument with my significant other. I was angry at the time and I must have blamed him for all that I could think of. I try not to go to bed angry because I know tomorrow is not promised. This however, is very difficult for me at times. I know Jesus has a way of communicating with me through my dreams. That night I prayed and ask God to speak to me. I couldn't sleep because my heart was troubled. When I did fall asleep that night Jesus sent a message to me in my dreams, "Judge not, and be not judged." I didn't realize it when I initially woke up but after a couple of hours I begin to understand his message. I was being extremely hard on my significant other, when all along I was just as guilty. A lot of times we are so selfish and worried about our own needs that we fail to see that we can actually be spending more of our time giving some of that same love to others. I learned that my expressive ways make it easy for others to know what I expect of them. However, some people are not as expressive as others (especially some men), therefore making it difficult to know if I have done or need to do something to heal the relationship. I learned that my outspoken ways can be painful to him at times. No one wants to constantly be reminded of things they are doing wrong, especially by people whom they love and cherish. We all have our faults. Many different in ways, yet we all have things in which we can do better. I'm learning today that the time I use complaining about what someone else isn't doing right, I can use to correct my faults. When you constantly talk about others and judge one another, someone somewhere is doing the same to you. If our sins are good enough for Jesus to forgive then who are we to constantly try to change others and point the finger? When you love someone, you love them for everything that they are. Faults, talents, dreams, goals and all. It's good to have someone who's willing to change for the better with you and grow with you. However, to ask someone to change for you is very selfish. We should change because we want to do it for ourselves, if it helps the relationship along the way, then glory to all. Change is good, change is necessary yet it should be an individual choice. It should not be used as a punching bag for your love one to throw in your face and make you feel bad. Like Jesus said, "Judge not and be not judged." We all need to change, we all struggle to find that narrow path, we all have had days that we did not feel as good as others. As people we are suppose to help uplift one another when he/she is weak. As sisters and brothers in Christ, Jesus wants us to love and lean on one another. Why must we judge, criticize and kick each other when we're down? Personally, I realized that as sinners, we do this without even thinking about it sometimes. "Why do you always do this, why do you always do that? Why did she wear that? Her face is huge and her legs are skinny. Who is that girl on your MySpace page? Who are you on the phone with?" Questions that is truly unnecessary. Questions that you ask when you assume you are truly a perfect person with no faults. Questions that you would not ask if you are being faithful in your relationship with others as well as yourself. I'm learning that you have to pick your battles. Many times we get upset and complain over simple things. However, someone somewhere else is dealing with problems that are beyond belief. I'm learning that my life and my career are my own and others walk a different path in life because that's all that they have or know. Who am I to judge someone's path in life? I need to worry about my ways, my habits and the things in which I choose to change and how the things I cannot change will affect my family and friends. For truly no one, including myself is and will ever be without sin. God is the only one without fault. Thank you GOD for continuing to speak to me and put me in my place as you ask all of your children, "If any one of you is without sin, let him be the first to throw a stone at her." This is not a prayer, but this is something for you to read and reflect on how we are so quick to do wrong and point the finger when all along we just need to cry out to God and he will renew our strength so we can pray. Reflect on these things today and ask God to renew your strength today. He is able.

When are we going to stop pointing
The finger and judging one another?
When are we going to start being truthful
And start trusting each other?
Is friendship just a phrase we use too
Freely throughout our life?
And why do married couples stumble
Taking on the role of husband and wife?
Why do we look at our brother and envy

His goods,
When he works twice as hard as we know
We should?
Why is it so easy to notice another's
Weakness so clear,
When all along we struggle in this life
And hide behind our own pain and tears?
When are we going to accept that each
Individual is different in his own way?
When will we see that nothing is
Impossible with God if we just
Reach out and pray?
When are we going to start helping
Build each other up inside,
Instead of tearing each other down
By backstabbing lies?
Why do we cheat on our lovers with
his/her friends?
Why are we happy when other
Couple's relationship comes to an end?
Why are we jealous hearted and always
Want what someone else possesses?
And when we know something may not
Be right for us, why do we say "yes"?
Why do women say a good man is hard
To find,
When they cheat on the ones God sends
Them time after time?
Why do men get hurt by one woman
And then forever cheat on the rest?
Why does life knock you off your feet
When you know you gave it your best?
Why do we give up so easily when
We are almost at the finish line?
And why is it that all the pretty

People have low self-esteem and
Get hurt every time?
Why is it that more couples separate
Right after they have kids?
Why does little mistakes hurt us
More, than mistakes really big?
As all of these things go through my
Mind, I can't help but to wonder why?
God said we may not understand it
Now, but we will by and by.
I just hope that we will learn
To have peace within our hearts.
Know that whatever you go
Through, be strong and don't let
It tears you apart.
Faith, hope and love. If we
Learn to live by the three,
Jesus promises a new beginning
For sinners like you and me.

Women of Christ

When I was 20 years old, I was living with my family in Houston TX. I wanted to move away and start a life of my own. I wanted to be able to say, I made a mistake, but it's my mistake that I made and I learned on my own. Being around family often, one does not get the space to think and be responsible for their own actions. April of 1999. That is exactly what I did. One of my biggest fears was flying. When I left to join the Military I had to fly to Great Lakes Illinois. As the plane took off, I knew that this was the first step of venturing out and taking control of my life. I took a deep breath as the plane took off and as I looked down the city of Houston begin to look smaller and smaller and eventually disappeared in the clouds.

When I was stationed on a ship USS JFK, my life begins to change and I knew I was growing up as a woman. I met my son's father on the ship.

We married

And had my son. Shortly thereafter we were divorce. During our marriage I made many mistakes as a woman that I can look back on now and say I was wrong. I stepped outside of our marriage and allowed insiders to tear our relationship apart. As a woman we are suppose to be the backbone when it comes to comfort and love. I was the total Opposite. Because of my reactions, he reflected the same. We were young and dumb. Before we married we cheated on one another also. I truly thought I knew what love was. I had a lot to learn about being a woman the years ahead. When I left the ship in Jacksonville, FL I was stationed in Atlanta Georgia. Atlanta showed me that there was some fire inside of me that I had to get out, and as a married woman, the time could not have been worse. My husband (at the time) was still on the ship that was deployed for 6 months two days after we married. I thought I could be strong and faithful but I was wrong. He was not the sentimental type so as far as emotionally; he was never really there anyway. I begin to hang out with the devil. I would drink and party with people who I called "shipmates and friends", little did I know the decisions I made caused me to stray away from the love of GOD. I found myself in the clubs all during the week. I couldn't get enough. I met a guy who I allowed to get inside of my head and that was the confirmation I needed to forget all about husband out to sea. Meanwhile, he was on the ship messing around with everyone he could get his hands on. Although I didn't know, that's just how life works. We both were weak in the flesh. I was not being faithful to my wifely duties at all. After I got divorced I had time to reflect on my life and the person I was without any disturbance. I thought I needed a man to complete me. I soon found out that God was all I needed. God was going to be that power I needed to restore my soul and help me be the kind of woman I needed to be most of all for myself and then for my child. My strength grew as I called upon his name. No matter what you are going through today ladies, Know that God is able and he will deliver you. There is no man alive that can replace the love and understanding of our Lord and Savior. We are all weak in the flesh, but God is able and he will do for us, what we can't do alone. A good man can be a great man with a Godly woman by his side. A good woman can be a great woman with intimate moments with God alone. When you feel alone ladies, know that God hands are open and all you have to do is come running in his word.

DEUTERONOMY 30:19

"I call Heaven and Earth a witnesses today against you, that I have set before you life and death, blessings and cursing; therefore choose life, that both you and your descendants may live."

DEAR GOD,

FOR YOUR WORD CLEARLY STATES THAT YOU HAVE GIVEN ME A CHOICE IN THIS LIFE.

I CAN CHOOSE THAT NARROW PATH, DOING WHAT IN MY HEART, I KNOW IS RIGHT.

FOR OFTEN TIMES WE STUMBLE AND IN THIS WORLD OF EVIL WE STRAY.

BUT BECAUSE YOUR WORD IS PLANTED IN MY SOUL, YOU BRING ME BACK YOUR WAY.

THANK YOU JESUS FOR BELIEVING IN ME, WHEN I WAS TOO FOOLISH TO BELIEVE IN MYSELF.

AS WOMEN, MANY TIMES WE LOOK FOR COMFORT IN THE WRONG PLACES, ONLY TO BE LEFT DAMAGED BY SOMEONE ELSE.

CONTINUE TO TEACH ME TO BE STRONG AND NOT BLAME OTHERS FOR MY DOWNFALLS.

TEACH ME THAT ONLY I CAN CONTROL MY LIFE AND BREAK DOWN THESE BRICK WALLS.

LORD GIVE ME THE WISDOM I NEED TO RAISE MY CHILD SO THAT HE WILL ALWAYS CALL UPON YOU,

BECAUSE I WILL NOT ALWAYS BE THERE, BUT WITH FAITH HE TOO WILL MAKE IT THROUGH.

FOR OFTEN TIMES WHEN WE ARE ALONE, WE ALLOW THE DEVIL TO SPEAK TO US IN DIFFERENT VOICES,

BUT I KNOW IF I KEEP MY EYES LIFTED TOWARDS THE HEAVENS,

YOU'LL GUIDE ME TO MAKE BETTER CHOICES.

THANK YOU JESUS FOR GIVING ME FREE WILL AND LOVING ME SO MUCH THAT YOU CONTINUE TO GIVE ME A SECOND TRY.

FOR THERE WERE TIMES WHEN I COULD NOT SEE THE ROAD AHEAD BUT YOU SAW FIT FOR ME TO LIVE INSTEAD OF DIE.

PLEASE HELP MYSELF AND MY SISTERS IN CHRIST UNDERSTAND,

THAT ONLY YOU CAN FILL THAT VOID IN OUR LIVES, SO WE MAY NOT BURDEN A MAN.

FOR YOU KNOW WHEN THE TIME IS RIGHT TO SEND PEOPLE IN AND OUT OF OUR LIVES, WHATEVER THE REASON.

FOR WE KNOW SOME COMES OUR WAY FOR A LIFETIME AND SOME FOR A SEASON.

YET WE ARE ALL HUMANS THAT HAVE AND WILL ALWAYS FALL SHORT OF SIN,

AND LIKE YOU FATHER, TEACH US TO FORGIVE ONE ANOTHER AND GIVE SECOND CHANCES AGAIN AND AGAIN.

THIS EARTHLY BATTLE IS ONGOING, FOR YOU SAID BEFORE FATHER,
"IF THEY PROSECUTE ME, THEY WILL ALSO PROSECUTE YOU"
AS I WATCH THE NEWS TODAY JESUS, TIME AND TIME AGAIN, THIS IS PROVEN TO BE TRUE.

AS WOMEN STANDING STRONG IN YOUR HOUSE, WE OFFER OUR HEARTS IN YOU CHRIST
THAT WE MAY CONTINUE TO GIVE,
FOR YOUR WORD CLEARLY STATES, "THEREFORE CHOOSE LIFE THAT BOTH YOU AND YOUR DESCENDANTS MAY LIVE".
AMEN

Worrying

LUKE 18: 40-42

*"So Jesus stood still and commanded him to be brought
to him. And when he had come near, he asked him
saying, what do you want me to do for you?*

*He said, Lord, that I may receive my sight.
Then Jesus said to him, Receive your sight; your faith
has made you well."*

As I think about this day when Jesus was passing near Jericho,
I am truly reminded that the same miracles he was doing
yesterday, he is doing today as well. It's just that many of us do
not call out to him and ask for our blessings. This blind man
cried out to Jesus and humbled himself before him because he
knew that all power was in his hands. Today our world is so
covered in sin and the truth of Jesus is not the main priority
in our media and in our schools as well as businesses. The
world is so busy they don't have time for the word of God.
The generation of tomorrow will not know if we don't spread

the news of Jesus. Praising Jesus all day. Thanking him for his mercy and realizing that we are nothing without his grace. All these things together will make a recipe for Faith. The kind of Faith that will not only help the blind to see, but the lame to walk, the poor to riches, the powerless to powerful, the hate to love, the mean to kind, the untrue to true, the fake to real, and the unbelievers to believers. The Faith of the word of God is power. There is power in the name of Jesus. I try to make it a habit to call on the name of Jesus. Jesus hears and sees all. When you call him, he's right there. Although we may not see him physically, we must know that he's there. All he asks is that we believe. The only way we can believe is through faith. Today he is truly asking the same question to us, "What do you want me to do for you?" I am a living testimony that sometimes we can be so blinded by the troubles of the world and so deep in sin that we don't hear Jesus voice when he ask us this question. Sometimes we hear only what we want to hear. Have you ever done something that you know was wrong, but you did it anyway? Something in the back of your mind was saying don't do it but you did it anyway? Well when we fall to this temptation then we can't hear Jesus. He is the truth and the light. No man comes to the father but through him. Someone who is full of truth and light does not deal with sins and wicked ways. When we choose to walk this path we separate ourselves from his love. For his word truly states that when we choose evil over good, "We will call to him and he will not answer." Many times we block our blessings when we fail to obey the commandments of God. God does not make exceptions for anyone. I know there were times I felt that I did so much good in a week that if I just did this one little thing then God probably would let me slide. Well I'm here to say, his word is the truth and nothing slides. The word is written, "You reap what you sew." It may not come to you in the exact fashion that you commit your sins, but it will come back to you and sometimes even worse. When we allow sin to rule over our souls the faith that we seek are hidden in the rubbles of our troubles. We have to work even harder to make that faith strong. When I stand on the word of Jesus and become steadfast in my walk with him, then the joy I receive from the Holy Spirit will multiply that faith in so many ways. I've learned that the devil knows our individual weakness. He knows what my failures and faults are and he preys on that. When you choose to walk with Jesus the devil stands closer to you than ever. He watches and he waits. Never glorifying him, but never under-estimate how desperate he can be to turn you away from the Savior. I say to all as well as myself as I continue this fight on earth, the devil can't touch you as long as you have the faith of Jesus on your side. He can look, he can talk, he can cry out, he can laugh, but the power of the faith of Jesus is untouchable. I'm learning that when you are a child of God, you don't have to open your mouth sometimes, you don't have to do anything, he will position others in your life to protect you and by your good deeds people will know that you are his child. When you are a child of God and you walk with your faith, sometimes you may not even know the danger you are or could be in, but he shelters you. You could be in the worse neighborhood, you could be in the mist of a fight, fire or hurricane, but if you believe and it is his will, God will bring you out. Trust him. Ask him. Love him. Humble yourself before him and know that you are nothing without his mercy and grace. As I said before, for we are of the earth so our way of thinking is earthly. Jesus is from Heaven and so his way of thinking is higher and heavenly. Therefore, we must know that life will throw things our way that we will never understand so we must have faith and know that Jesus is working it out for us. Ask him for understanding, believe and receive. "Faith is the substance of all things hoped for, and the evidence of all things not seen." In a world full of sin and temptation, it's just so good to know that the same Jesus that passed a blind man's way so long ago, is still walking by me today with arms wide open saying, "What do you want me to do for you?" I wrote this poem for the students at Georgia Tech who was killed on that fatal day. God is good and he listens even when the world forget us. Although he may not answer us the way in which we want him to, he said his mercy and grace is sufficient. Pray this prayer for your strength in God when you worry about the problems of this world. God is able.

MATTHEW 6:34

"Therefore do not worry about tomorrow, for tomorrow will worry about itself. Each day has enough trouble of its own."

DEAR GOD,
   PLEASE HELP OUR COUNTRY IN THIS TIME OF NEED AND HEARTACHE.
   ONCE AGAIN TRAGEDY HAS TAKEN US BY SURPRISE BY AN ACT OF EVIL SO FIERCE AND SO GREAT.

   FOR MANY OF US MAY NOT UNDERSTAND TODAY HOW A PLACE THAT IS SUPPOSE TO BE SAFE AND SOUND,
   A LEARNING INSTITUTION, A PLACE OF KNOWLEDGE, VIRGINIA TECH'S CAMPUS GROUND.

   BUT WE KNOW EVERYTHING HAPPENS FOR A REASON,
   AND IN DUE TIME WE ALL WILL HAVE OUR OWN DESTINY, OUR INDIVIDUAL SEASON.

   FATHER WE JUST ASK THAT YOU COMFORT THOSE FAMILY MEMBERS AND FRIENDS AS THEY TRY TO COPE WITH THIS LOSS.

HELP THEM TO SEE NOW THEIR LOVE ONES CAN LIVE IN ETERNAL HEAVEN BECAUSE YOUR SON PAID THE ULTIMATE COST.

GOD HELP US ALL, MEN, WOMEN, BOYS AND GIRLS,
TO LIVE FOR TODAY IN THIS UNPREDICTABLE WORLD.

SHOW US THE IMPORTANT OF TAKING A LITTLE EXTRA CASH TO BUY HER THAT BRAND NEW DRESS,
AND ALTHOUGH SCHOOL AND WORK IS IMPORTANT, WATCH THE SUNSET OFTEN TO RELAX AND REST.

SHOW THOSE LIVING IN WASHINGTON D.C. THAT IF THEY EVER GET A CHANCE TO GO TO THE CHERRY BLOSSOM FESTIVAL IN APRIL IT'S GREAT!
GO OVERSEAS FOR SPRING BREAK AND START GETTING YOUR HOTEL FOR MARDI GRAS-DON'T WAIT!

FATHER, HELP US TO LOVE ONE ANOTHER AS YOU HAVE LOVED US FROM THE FIRST DAY.
FOR YOU SAID THAT IS THE GREATEST GIFT WE CAN GIVE, SO PLEASE TEACH US YOU'RE WAYS.

WHEN WE WAKE UP IN THE MORNING AND THINGS SEEM TO BE GOING GOOD.
HELP US TO PRAY FOR INSPIRATION THROUGHOUT THE DAY LIKE WE SHOULD.

IF EACH ONE OF US PRAYS FOR SOMEBODY, WE MAY SPARE SOMEONE HEARTACHE AND PAIN.

HELP US TO STOP WORRYING ABOUT THINGS WE CAN'T CHANGE BUT LET

US LEARN HOW TO STOP MAKING THE SAME MISTAKES OVER AND OVER AGAIN.

MOST OF ALL, HELP US TO STOP PUTTING OFF TOMORROW WHAT WE CAN DO TODAY ALL BECAUSE WE MAY THINK THE TIMING IS WRONG,

FOR IN YOUR WORDS YOU SAID,

"Therefore do not worry about tomorrow, for tomorrow will worry about itself. Each day has enough trouble of its own."

AMEN

I Wish I'd Known Jesus

Have you ever longed to be like the superstars on TV? Women have you ever wanted to be skinny and beautiful like the ladies in the magazines? Men have you ever wanted to be like the super heroes in the cartoons who could save the world? You ever wanted to be the man that everyone looked at as the super hero? Well when you become a child of God, when you start to mature in the word of God, the things in which you desire begin to shift. When you find yourself wanting to be more like Jesus, when you find yourself wanting to encourage other people, when you find yourself wanting to grow in the spirit of the Lord and read his word, you are growing as a Christian. That's good news. Let your thoughts be pleasant, reach high for Goals that will be pleasing to the Lord. Sometimes we know we may never be able to make people as happy as we wish we could, but never loose that desire to do so. Jesus was an awesome man. God put him in the flesh so that he may know what we go through everyday, yet and still he kept his purpose in the Lord. That is why we can stand and be mighty today. I wish I was in a room with him when I was younger. Maybe I might have gained some of that wisdom. I wish I could have told others, that I was his classmate. Do you wish good thoughts of God or do you wish thoughts that are pleasing to man? Read this poem for inspiration in the Lord as you seek thoughts that reflect your maturity in the word today. Pray that God will help you glorify him even in your thoughts. God is able.

I WISH I'D KNOWN JESUS
WHEN HE WAS JUST A LITTLE BOY.
WE WOULD BE BEST FRIENDS THAT
SHARED EACH OTHER'S TOYS.
OUR MOTHERS WOULD HAVE BEEN
NEIGHBORS THAT LIVED ACROSS
THE STREET.
OFTEN TIMES WE WOULD INVITE
THEM OVER FOR DINNER,
OR PERHAPS GO OUT TO EAT.

I WISH I'D KNOWN JESUS
WHEN HE WAS JUST A YOUNG CHILD.
WE WOULD RIDE HORSES TOGETHER
LIKE THE COWBOYS OF THE OLD WILD.
I'D LIKE TO THINK WE WOULD
CLIMB TREES AND WATCH THE SUN
GO DOWN.
WE WOULD LOOK OUT FOR ONE ANOTHER
WHEN OUR PARENTS WERE NOT AROUND.

I WISH I'D KNOWN JESUS WHEN HE WAS
JUST A LITTLE KID.
MY SISTER AND BROTHER WOULD
CHERISH HIM JUST AS MUCH AS I DID.
AT NIGHT HE WOULD TEACH
US HOW TO PRAY.
WHEN HE WOULD CRY,
I WOULD WIPE HIS TEARS AWAY.
SWEET WOULD BE THE REFLECTION OF OUR

LOVE,
SHOWING OTHERS WHAT HEAVEN
IS MADE OF.

OF ALL THE PEOPLE IN THE WORLD
THAT WE KNOW WOULD GLADLY PLEASE US.
I WISH I MIGHT HAVE KNOWN HIM,
BEFORE HE WAS JESUS.